BFI FILM CL/

Rob Whi
SERIES ED

Colin MacCabe and David Meeker
SERIES CONSULTANTS

Cinema is a fragile medium. Many of the great classic films of the past now exist, if at all, in damaged or incomplete prints. Concerned about the deterioration in the physical state of our film heritage, the National Film and Television Archive, a Division of the British Film Institute, has compiled a list of 360 key films in the history of the cinema. The long-term goal of the Archive is to build a collection of perfect showprints of these films, which will then be screened regularly at the Museum of the Moving Image in London in a year-round repertory.

BFI Film Classics is a series of books commissioned to stand alongside these titles. Authors, including film critics and scholars, film-makers, novelists, historians and those distinguished in the arts, have been invited to write on a film of their choice, drawn from the Archive's list. Each volume presents the author's own insights into the chosen film, together with a brief production history and a detailed filmography, notes and bibliography. The numerous illustrations have been specially made from the Archive's own prints.

With new titles published each year, the BFI Film Classics series will rapidly grow into an authoritative and highly readable guide to the great films of world cinema.

Could scarcely be improved upon ... informative, intelligent, jargon-free companions.
The Observer

Cannily but elegantly packaged BFI Classics will make for a neat addition to the most discerning shelves.
New Statesman & Society

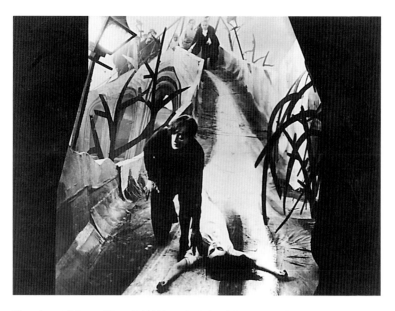

The exhausted Cesare (Conrad Veidt) lays down the abducted Jane (Lil Dagover)

BFI FILM

C L A S S I C S

DAS CABINET DES
DR. CALIGARI

. . . .

David Robinson

 Publishing

First published in 1997 by the
BRITISH FILM INSTITUTE
21 Stephen Street, London W1P 2LN

AG 1 9 '09

Copyright © David Robinson 1997
Reprinted 1999, 2002, 2004, 2005
The British Film Institute exists
to promote appreciation, enjoyment, protection and
development of moving image culture in and throughout the
whole of the United Kingdom.
Its activities include the National Film and
Television Archive; the National Film Theatre;
the Museum of the Moving Image;
the London Film Festival; the production and
distribution of film and video; funding and support for
regional activities; Library and Information Services;
Stills, Posters and Designs; Research;
Publishing and Education; and the monthly
Sight and Sound magazine.

British Library Cataloguing-in-Publication Data
A catalogue record for this book is available from the British Library

ISBN 0–85170–645–2

Designed by
Andrew Barron & Collis Clements Associates

Typesetting by
D R Bungay Associates, Burghfield, Berks.

Printed in Great Britain by Norwich Colour Printers

CONTENTS

. . . .

1

. . . .

THE MAKING OF 'CALIGARI'
'The Story of a Famous Story' Revised

Das Cabinet des Dr. Caligari, whose arrival so neatly and precisely coincided with the end of the first quarter of the cinema's first century, was in many respects a landmark in film history. The wonder film of 1920 indicated new aesthetic ambitions for the cinema; new relationships between film and the graphic arts, between actor and setting, between image and narrative. The links it established between the still infant cinema and the most progressive art movements of the day startled and attracted an intellectual public which until then had rarely paid attention to a still dubious area of show business. Moreover it brought German film culture unprecedented international prestige, and helped to reopen overseas markets which had been closed since the World War and the economic ostracism that followed. *Caligari* was unique, unprecedented. The story of its genesis has in consequence a particular fascination.

Over the years, however, that story has been obfuscated by an accumulation of legend and conflicting evidence. As *Das Cabinet des Dr. Caligari* itself was elevated to a mythical place in the history of cinema and of twentieth-century culture in general, people associated with it sought to emphasise and dramatise their own contributions to the film. For those artists driven into exile after the advent of Nazism, and obliged to remake their careers in alien countries, it was often especially important to be able to stake a claim in the creating of *Caligari*, an infallible calling-card.

The essay which follows attempts to sift and balance those claims and to arrive at a clearer idea of how *Das Cabinet des Dr. Caligari* came to be made at that time and by those people. Particularly it is concerned to assess the contribution of the credited director of the film, Robert Wiene, who, as the first casualty of the group that made the film (he died in 1938) had less chance than the others to assert his role in the work. Such revaluation of the production history is made possible by the rediscovery of documents – the original script; the contract with the writers; some scattered testimonies – which have been unknown to or disregarded by most earlier commentators.

The Writers

For almost fifty years the received version of the story of the film's making has been that set down by Dr Siegfried Kracauer in 1947 in his influential book *From Caligari to Hitler: A Psychological History of the German Film*.[1] Kracauer based his account largely on an unpublished typescript entitled 'Caligari: The Story of a Famous Story', by Hans Janowitz, one of the film's two scenarists.[2] It is not altogether surprising then that the Kracauer–Janowitz version gives principal credit for *Caligari* to the writers. Janowitz, in 'Caligari: The Story of a Famous Story' remained adamant that

> The actual 'architects' of *Caligari*, from the conception of the idea to the last line of the shooting script, were the two authors and no one else.
>
> Even the innovation of having the sets painted on canvas, instead of using the customary scenery, may be found in the directions of the shooting script of the two authors.

As we shall see, subsequent evidence – notably the rediscovery of the original script to which Janowitz so confidently refers – today obliges us to take a cautious view of the Kracauer–Janowitz version.

Hans Janowitz was born in Podebrand, Böhmen in 1890, and spent his early years in Prague. A precocious and prolific writer, he published

his first short story at seventeen, was a theatre critic at the age of eighteen and a dramaturge and occasional actor at the Hamburg Schauspielhaus at twenty-two. He had early encounters with Expressionism, contributing to Max Brod's Prague-published Expressionist review *Arkadia*. On the outbreak of war in 1914 he volunteered for the Austrian army and reached the rank of Captain. His service experiences led him to a fierce detestation of war, which was intensified after the death on the Italian front of

Hans Janowitz (Stiftung Deutsche Kinemathek)

his beloved younger brother Franz in 1917.[3] After the war Janowitz enthusiastically committed himself to the short-lived German revolution, and wrote for some of the left-wing and revolutionary cultural magazines that proliferated at that time.

Janowitz recalled that he was on army leave in 1918 when the actor Ernst Deutsch, a friend from his Prague youth, introduced him to Carl Mayer (1894–1944). Mayer, according to Janowitz's characteristically over-coloured account, was the son of a rich Austrian merchant who squandered his entire fortune on gambling and eventually committed suicide. When Carl was sixteen, this improvident father gave him a small sum of money and turned him out into the street with his three younger brothers, for whom he was thereafter obliged to take full responsibility. The boy lived by a variety of odd jobs before becoming a bit-player in theatres and eventually rising to be dramaturge, writer, director and designer.

Janowitz claimed that Mayer spent much of the war years in a battle of wits with an army psychiatrist, successfully convincing him that he was mentally deranged, so that he could not be forced to fight in a war which he regarded as criminally insane. This psychiatrist, wrote Janowitz, became a model for Caligari: 'He represented the authoritative pressure that was brought to bear upon the powerless young man'. A subsequent biographer, Rolf Hempel,[4] offers the more prosaic version that Mayer was actually called up for infantry service, but was discharged after a day as unfit, on account of a foot injury suffered in childhood. (Hempel acknowledges though that Mayer's 'acting ability' may have enhanced the impact of this infirmity at the medical examination.)

In June 1918 Mayer introduced Janowitz, then still serving in the army, to the actress Gilda

Carl Mayer (Stiftung Deutsche Kinemathek)   9

Langer, with whom Mayer was in love and who was to be the inspiration for the character of Jane in *Caligari*. Janowitz saw a romantic fatalism in their meeting: Gilda was in mourning for her fiancé who had been killed on the Western front; Janowitz had just lost his soldier brother.

As Janowitz recorded, Gilda suggested that he and Mayer should collaborate: 'You are a poet; he is a dramaturge, you should write a film-story together.' Janowitz further claimed that she persuaded him to consult a fortune teller, who predicted that he would return safe from the war, but that Gilda would die. Both predictions came true – inspiring, said Janowitz, the scene in *Das Cabinet des Dr. Caligari* where the somnambulist Cesare foretells the death of Alan.

Janowitz and Mayer began work on their script in the winter of 1918–19, during the last weeks of the German revolution (Rosa Luxemburg and Carl Liebknecht, leading left-wing activists, were murdered by the right-wing Freikorps in January 1919). Looking back, more than twenty years later, Janowitz considered that his distinctive contributions to the conception were fourfold. First, the atmosphere of mystery inspired by memories of his home-town Prague. Second, the sense of foreboding he had already demonstrated in his play *Prager Fastnachtsspiel um 1913* (1913). Third, the inspiration of a bizarre incident which he witnessed in Hamburg in 1913: at an amusement park on the Reeperbahn, beside the Holstenwall, he had noticed a young girl, 'drunken with the happiness of life'. Fascinated, he followed her, but she disappeared into some bushes, from which emerged, moments later, an unremarkable bourgeois man. Next day he learned that the girl had been murdered. The incident left an indelible impression: the created town in *Das Cabinet des Dr. Caligari* is called 'Holstenwall'. Finally, and most important in Janowitz's view, was the pathological mistrust of 'the authoritative power of an inhuman state gone mad' which he had acquired through five and a half years of military service.

The specific story of *Caligari* was suggested by a sideshow featuring a hypnotised strong man, which the writers saw together in an amusement park on Berlin's Kantstrasse, their favourite evening haunt.

After six weeks' work they finished the script, which Janowitz remembered as consisting of 168 scenes. Not until the scenario was practically complete did the authors decide on the name of the main character: both were delighted with 'Caligari', which Janowitz claimed he discovered in 'a rare book ... called *Unknown Letters of Stendhal*',[5] where it appeared as the name of an Italian officer whom Stendhal had encountered at the Scala Theatre, Milan. Caligari's physical appearance, wrote Janowitz, was modelled on portraits of Schopenhauer.

Since both writers were penniless at the time, they were in a hurry to sell their script. At some time, through Fritz Lang, Janowitz had met Erich Pommer, then head of production at the Decla-Bioscop company, who had casually suggested that Janowitz should try writing a script. According to Pommer's account, the two knocked on his office door one afternoon, and resisted all his attempts to get rid of them. When he asked them to leave the script with him, they refused, insisting that Mayer must read it aloud there and then.[6] Pommer gave in, and he and his assistant Julius Sternheim sat and listened attentively. 'The four of us smoked steadily, not, as might be suspected, the cigarettes of the Decla Picture Corporation – Oh no – but our own! That hurt!', Janowitz recalled.

Pommer was so impressed that he would not let the writers leave the office until a contract had been signed. The script was bought and paid for by eight o'clock the same evening. Mayer and Janowitz had decided in advance that their minimum price was ten thousand marks, but settled for 4,000.[7]

The written contract, now preserved in the Bundesfilmarchiv, Berlin, is dated 19 April 1919, and gives the producer the right to make any changes to the script that 'sooner or later' may seem desirable. The writers moreover agree to help with any such changes and to provide written material for an eventual advertising brochure, without further charge. A clause that seems to have been added after the brief main text was typed, and which is further amended in manuscript, specifies that the authors' names shall be mentioned on the film and in all advertising.

The wily Pommer later explained his alacrity in accepting the script: 'The mysterious and macabre atmosphere of Grand Guignol was at the time in vogue in German films, and this story was perfectly full of it. They saw in their script an "Experiment" – I saw a comparatively inexpensive production.'

Pommer recalls that there was a delay of four or five months before the film went into production. Fritz Lang was initially assigned to direct the film, but was taken off the project in order to prepare the second part of his serial *Die Spinnen* (*The Spiders*). (Strangely, Janowitz makes no mention of Lang's involvement, though in 1970 Lang recalled that his preparatory discussions about the script were exclusively with

Janowitz: only much later did he learn that Mayer was co-author.[8])
Robert Wiene, some of whose scripts – notably for Murnau's three-part
Satanas – had already demonstrated a predilection for the fantastic,[9]
took over the project.

How closely the writers were involved during the production
period is disputed. Janowitz boasted in 'Caligari: The Story of a Famous
Story' that Wiene

> had a difficult time with us, the two authors. In our opinion the
> script could not be improved and the cast, with Werner Krauss as
> Caligari, Conrad Veidt as Cesare and Twardowski as the student,
> we had selected and therefore considered good.

(Janowitz however had originally planned the part of Cesare for his
friend Ernst Deutsch. The role of Jane had been designed for Gilda
Langer, but now she was dead, they settled for Lil Dagover, who was
suitably beautiful and mysterious.) 'Nor', Janowitz emphasises, 'would
we discuss any proposed change in the script, as we believed that any
change would hamper its careful structure.'

According to Pommer's (generally unreliable) testimony, Carl
Mayer was on the set every day, 'a habit which Mayer maintained
throughout his film career'. However, Hermann Warm, who as chief
designer was certainly at the studio throughout the entire shooting,
remembered that

> The writers Carl Mayer and Hans Janowitz never appeared in the
> studio during the preparation or shooting, or took part in any
> discussions.
>
> Nor was Erich Pommer ever at any discussion. I was
> astonished that this last-named gentleman showed no interest in
> such an unusual production; [Rudolph] Meinert later explained to
> me that he had not sanctioned the style of the film.[10]

That Janowitz and Mayer were not regularly present at the filming of
their script seems to be confirmed by Janowitz's version of the
circumstances in which Decla came to make what the writers felt was a
fundamental and deeply damaging change to their conception. In the
finished film, the main narrative is related as a flashback from a framing

scene set in a madhouse. The story of the monstrous Caligari, a psychiatrist masquerading as a showman, who uses his creature, the hypnotised somnambulist Cesare, to commit murders, is thus presented as the fantasy of a deranged asylum patient. This change, Janowitz wrote in 'Caligari: The Story of a Famous Story', was

> dishonoring our drama – the tragedy of a man, gone mad by the misuse of his mental powers – into a cliché, in which the symbolism was to be lost.

Janowitz makes clear that neither he nor Mayer was present at any prior discussions of this revision:

> When we came to learn of this plan, we strongly protested. In vain. Then we instructed our attorneys to take the proper steps against this crime. But Wiene succeeded in having his version of the script approved by the production department.

It seems safe to suppose that the writers were also not present when the framing scenes were shot and edited into the film, since Janowitz states that it was only at a preview of the finished film for the studio heads that he and Mayer saw that the framing device had been used. Wiene stayed away from this preview, evidently fearing an outburst from the enraged writers, and indeed, said Janowitz,

> Carl Mayer and I both expressed our dissatisfaction in a storm of thunderous remonstrances, heaped upon the guilty heads of the persons in charge of production and upon the absent director.
> Mayer was raging and I, too, did not withhold my contempt for the impertinent blunderers who had put our drama into a 'box' that obscured its clarity.

They were dissuaded from a public protest, but in 1941 Janowitz still considered the change 'an illicit violation, a raping of our work'.

The Script
When Janowitz and Kracauer wrote, respectively in 1941 and 1947, when both were exiles in America, it was supposed that no copy of the

script for *Das Cabinet des Dr. Caligari* had survived. In the early 1950s, however, Werner Krauss – Dr. Caligari himself – told the critic Lotte Eisner that he still possessed his copy. Krauss refused absolutely to let it out of his hands and not until 1978, long after his death, did the Stiftung Deutsche Kinemathek succeed in buying the script from his widow.

Surprisingly, little attention seems to have been paid to the document, outside the Kinemathek itself, during the next seventeen years. Not until the end of 1995, when the Kinemathek published a full transcript, did this crucial document in cinema history become readily available. As late as 1990, the contributors to Mike Budd's substantial critical anthology *The Cabinet of Dr. Caligari: Texts, Contexts, Histories* seemed generally to be unaware of its existence. Budd himself accords the document two paragraphs, but confidently concludes that it is only 'an early script ... clearly not the final shooting script'.[11]

Budd's presumption is at first sight not unreasonable, given the significant differences instantly apparent both between the script and the finished film and between the script and Janowitz's memories of it. The natural first reaction is that this can only be a preliminary draft, of which later revisions are now lost.

This assumption might seem to be further supported by the physical character of the script – the inaccurate typing, the corrections, emendations and passages of manuscript additions, in two different hands.[12] (The actual document is a duplicate produced by some reproductive technique of the period).

Yet all other evidence overwhelmingly indicates that this represents the first, the last, and the only version of the *Caligari* script. By Janowitz's account, the original script was written in a mere six weeks. Both writers were so penniless that (Janowitz claimed) they had pawned their silver cigarette cases in order to eat. There was unlikely then to have been time or money to re-type the script. Further evidence that the surviving document is the writers' original version is the tentative form of character names. Caligari appears as Calligaris, though the final 's' has been deleted in some but not all occurrences; Cesare is Caesare; Alan is Allan (sometimes Alland); Franzis is Dr. Francis; Jane's father, Dr Olfen in the film, is Dr Olfens; the house-breaker or rogue, unnamed in the finished film, is identified as 'Jakob Straat'; the town clerk of Holstenwall is 'Dr. Lüders'.

Clearly subsequent to its acquisition by Decla the script has been supplied with a pictorial title page designed and signed by Walter Reimann, one of the three designers of the eventual film. The title on this cover is neatly lettered DAS CABINETT DES DR. CALLIGARI, the same orthographic form as the title-page of the typescript. The illustration shows a crowd in front of the fairground booth, where Caligari is displaying Cesare. Over the booth is written 'Der Somnambule Mensch'. That the studio took the trouble to prepare this cover, and that Reimann designed it, indicates that the script in this version still remained current during the design and pre-production stage.

Moreover, since it was in the possession of Werner Krauss, this is presumably the very copy that was given to him, as he recalls in his memoirs, a day or so before he began work on the film.

Janowitz's memoirs also seem implicitly to corroborate that the shooting script as delivered to the cast on the eve of shooting was the same as he and Mayer had originally brought to Pommer. Despite the contractual obligation to work on any required changes, he insisted, as we have seen, that in our opinion the script could not be improved ... Nor would we discuss any proposed change in the script, as we believed that any change would hamper its careful structure.

Yet if this is the one and only Mayer–Janowitz script, the discrepancies between the script and the film and between the script and Janowitz's categorical memory of it, twenty-one years after the event, are striking.

Janowitz unequivocally states that the finished script consisted of 168 scenes; in fact it has only 141 scenes. He boasts that

> We hit upon a new method of writing such a picture so that in being read to someone, scene after scene would project itself before the mind's eye of the listener. Every word, therefore, had to be weighed carefully as it had to release an association with a mental picture in the imagination of the listener and, at the same time, serve the continuity of the story. Nothing, nothing whatever, was to be permitted that was unnecessary, words and pictures had to coincide perfectly. The placing of every word was to be decided according to the importance of the visual impression it was meant to create.

This is an accurate description of the 'expressionist' style associated with the subsequent script work of Carl Mayer. Yet that style is by no means apparent in the *Caligari* script. Pommer himself noted particularly that '*The Cabinet of Dr. Caligari* can not be called a typical Carl Mayer scenario, though it served to lead him into his true medium.'[15]

The characteristic later Mayer style – truly 'Expressionist' with its vivid telegraphic bursts – can be seen in his script for Murnau's *Tartuffe* (1925):

49.
Closer shot: The first floor.
   Darkness of night.
   But! Descending the first flight of
              stairs;
      like a shadow; at first unrecognisable.
   Tartuffe?
      It is. He stands.

of the actors, so that the screen picture and the dramatic action, the mood and the psychological development of the story would have continuity, character and credibility.

To us, a picture-story had to be a straitjacket for the director ... Carl Mayer was master of this unusual technique of brain-photography ...

The description of the first appearance of Dr. Caligari anticipates the precision with which later Mayer scripts specified performance:

A spectral-looking old man, in a dark, flying cloak and high cylinder hat, trots along the street, following the procession. His hands, clasped behind his back, hold a walking stick. His head recalls that of Schopenhauer. He stands still for a moment, and before going on, solemnly leafs through the pages of a large book which he takes out of his coat pocket. Then he appears satisfied and goes on his way.

Later in the story, too,

Entering, Allan lights the oil lamp, which dimly illuminates the room. He takes off his coat and hat, and goes to the window, where he stretches, and reaches out into the night air, with a movement as if he would, with this gesture, sum up the long day. Then he shuts the window, closes the curtains and prepares to go to bed.

Mayer was to become the most celebrated advocate of a kind of cinema that should be totally expressive, without the need for expository titles: his script for Murnau's *The Last Laugh* is famous for dispensing with narrative titles altogether. Hence it is surprising to find in the *Caligari* script many titles that seem superfluous, duplicating the visible action. Others are much more wordy than in the finished film, where they appear to have been severely – and beneficially – edited. In the script, for example, Caligari is introduced by the title, attributed to Francis:

TITLE: In this retinue there was that mysterious man.

With much more dramatic effect, the finished film uses the single word, 'Er...' ('Him ...')

Design

Most strikingly, the script nowhere anticipates the singular visual experiment which was to earn the film its lasting fame. The description of Francis's country house, given above, or of Holstenwall ('An old German city, silhouetted in evening light ... old twisted, crooked streets') suggests no more than the 'Biedermeier' manner of pre-war fantasy films like *The Student of Prague*, which we know Janowitz admired.

Certainly nothing in the script supports Janowitz's assertion that 'the innovation of having the sets painted on canvas, instead of using the customary scenery, may be found in the directions of the shooting script ... as a matter of fact I, myself, wrote them in the original script, in the following words: "The scenery is to be designed in the style of Kubin's paintings"'. No such phrase appears in the script. Pommer, it is true, recollected a quarter of a century later that Janowitz and Mayer told him the film had to be done in 'a distinctive style. The artist whose style they wanted to follow was Alfred Kubin, the hero of Prague's radical artists'. Like Janowitz a native of Prague, Kubin (1877–1959) was known for his visionary, chiaroscuro fantasies of the city's Mediaeval streets.[13] Janowitz stated that he sent a telegram to Kubin, but that the painter declined to

collaborate on the grounds he was too busy. Meanwhile however, Janowitz alleged, someone at Decla, ignorant of Kubin's work, misread 'Kubinische' as 'Kubistische' and thereupon hired 'two young, accomplished painters, Hans Reiman and Hermann Roehrig' (was it lingering annoyance that caused Janowitz, writing in 1941, to mistake the names of Walter Reimann and Walter Röhrig?). The story would be a tall one, even if the word 'Kubinische' had actually appeared in the script, as Janowitz asserted.

Janowitz's claim that he and Mayer suggested the visual

style is even more conclusively contradicted by a series of articles by Barnet Braverman – a journalist known by Griffith scholars as a meticulous collector of first-hand testimonies – that appeared in *Billboard* and was subsequently reprinted in the 1926 *Film Year Book* (New York):

> When the scenario for *Caligari* was first handed to Wiene, the manuscript specified none of the style that appeared in the production. In form, the original scenario was conventional. But Wiene saw an opportunity for getting away from the customary by giving the scenes in *Caligari* settings and forms which intensified the thoughts and emotions of the characters and established a very positive relation between them and mimetic action. The authors did not want expressionist setting and decoration. To this day they do not understand why the picture had success. Mayer, one of its authors (who later wrote the scenario for *The Last Laugh*), has come round to Wiene's attitude; the other (Hans Janowitz) still insists that Wiene should never have handled the production of *Caligari* in the abstract style he gave it.

Paul Rotha appended this passage from Braverman as a footnote to his enthusiastic account of *Das Cabinet des Dr. Caligari* in *The Film Till Now*.[14] Since Rotha was Mayer's closest friend in the writer's last years, he had the opportunity to check the authority of this statement; and it is significant that he kept it unchanged throughout the various revisions of his book.

If then the idea was not anticipated by the writers, who was responsible for giving *Caligari* its distinctive visual style – thereby transforming it from a scenario that might easily have been forgotten along with the scores of mystery and crime thrillers of the time, into a milestone of film history? Decades after the event, of course, everyone wanted to take credit for the triumphant innovation of the Expressionist decors. In 1947, Erich Pommer, who according to Meinert had even 'not sanctioned' the style of the film, boldly claimed, 'In the meantime I … put *Caligari* into the hands of the three artists who composed Decla's designing staff.'[15] Pommer thereupon undermines his claim by incorrectly identifying the designers as Hermann Warm, Walter Röhrig and Robert Herlth, instead of Warm, Röhrig and Reimann.

The most convincing account of the visual conception of *Das Cabinet des Dr. Caligari* remains that of the chief designer Hermann

Warm. Writing in the 1960s,[16] when he and Lil Dagover were the only survivors from the film, Warm was apparently impelled to set down his recollections out of irritation at the accumulation of legend and competing claims of authorship.

Warm had no doubt that production credit for the film belonged to Rudolph Meinert, already known as an actor and director when he took over from Pommer as production head of Decla between mid–1919 and mid–1920 – a period which embraced the entire production and release period of the film (and a reasonable explanation for Pommer's absence from the production). *Das Cabinet des Dr. Caligari*, says Warm, represented the high point of Meinert's career: 'I would like at this point to thank production leader Meinert, for producing the Caligari film despite the opposition of a part of the management of Decla'.[17]

In the late autumn of 1919, Warm had just finished his work as designer of Fritz Lang's *Die Spinnen*, which preceded *Caligari* in Decla's Lixie-Atelier at Weissensee.[18] Meinert handed him the screenplay of *Caligari* in the presence of Robert Wiene – it was the first time the designer and director had met – and asked him to come back the following

day with proposals for the design. Reading the script the same afternoon, Warm found that 'the strange atmosphere of this very unusual script inspired me more and more ... The film images had to be removed from reality, had to have a fantastic, graphic style'. Warm consulted with Reimann and Röhrig, painters who had recently been working with him, also in the Lixie-Atelier, on Otto Rippert's *Pest in Florenz*, written by Fritz Lang. The collaboration had worked out well: the critics wrote that even someone who knew Florence well might believe that they were seeing the real thing, not studio sets. Warm

Hermann Warm (Stiftung Deutsche Kinemathek)

recalled that the three of them spent much of the night reading and discussing the *Caligari* script:

> Finally Reimann, whose paintings followed the technique of the expressive artists, won me round to his opinion that this theme called for an Expressionist style in decor, costume, acting and direction.

The painters spent the rest of the night roughing out designs in the Expressionist style, which they presented the following day to Wiene and Meinert. Warm recalled that Wiene approved instantly, but Meinert asked for twenty-four hours to think about it. The following day he too gave his approval, persuaded by cynical pragmatism rather than aesthetic ideals:

> He wanted the style and production to appear crazy … as crazy as could be. The film would then be a success as a sensation, regardless of whether the press turned out negative or positive, whether the critics killed it or praised it as art – either way the experiment would be in profit.[19]

Cesare abducts Jane

The decision thus made, the artists set to work. Warm recalls that the designs and ordering of construction, costumes and props took a week and a half or two weeks. So far as possible sets were prepared to permit the film to be shot in story sequence. Shooting began at the end of December 1919 and lasted till the end of January 1920.

2

. . . .

'CALIGARI', THE FILM

Scenario and Film

The collaborator to whom historical legend has given least credit for *Das Cabinet des Dr. Caligari* is its director, Robert Wiene. Paradoxically, *Caligari* may in the long run have done more to efface than to enhance Wiene's reputation. Without this spectacular highlight to his career, he would be remembered as one of the superior craftsmen of early German cinema, seen at his best in *Orlacs Hände* and some of his films with Henny Porten; Walter Kaul characterises him as 'a man of artistic taste and tact'.[20] *Caligari*, though, eclipsed all the rest; and when Wiene was unable ever to match its success – two subsequent 'Expressionist' efforts, *Genuine* and *Raskolnikov* failed to repeat the trick – he was forever written off as a one-film director who had a lucky fluke with *Caligari*.

The myth set down by Janowitz, propagated by Kracauer and accepted, more or less without question, by every writer since, is that Mayer and Janowitz gave Wiene a finished script that 'in our opinion ...

2 4   Robert Wiene (centre) with, on his right, Conrad Veidt, *c.* 1923

could not be improved'. In the role of director, Robert Wiene had only to realise what was written, dutifully and perhaps, it was often patronisingly suggested, uncomprehendingly. Comparison between scenario and film suggest that this view of the production circumstances is at best misleading.

The surviving scenario is a detailed shooting script of a kind that was certainly unusual, if not unique, at the time. Film-makers of the early 1920s generally worked only from a broad story treatment, with most of the creative process happening on the set. In the case of *Caligari*, many of the writers' detailed suggestions have indeed been accepted totally – most notably the curious and effective use of constant fade-ins and fade-outs ('abblenden', 'aufblenden') between and often within scenes. Yet equally, the film reveals substantial divergences from the script, which can be studied in detail in the Appendix to this book.

Since it seems safe to suppose that the surviving Mayer–Janowitz scenario served as the actual shooting script for the film, and that Janowitz and Mayer themselves took little or no part in the practical filming process, we must regard and assess the changes from script to screen as the contribution of Robert Wiene, his crew and the uncredited editor (most likely Wiene himself, in accordance with then current film-making practice).

These changes are of three kinds: practical, demanded by the production conditions; visual, consequent on the decision to use the stylised design; and dramaturgical.

Practical changes were clearly dictated by the condition that the film was entirely shot in the studio. At the time it was unusual for any film to dispense entirely with exterior location shots: in this case, however, studio shooting followed inevitably from the fundamental decision to give the film its stylised, 'Expressionist' look.

The glass-house Lixie-Atelier at Weissensee, originally built for Vitascope GmbH in 1913, was restrictive in scale. (*Caligari* was the fourth Decla production made there, following *Die Pest in Florenz* and the two parts of Lang's *Die Spinnen*.) The *Caligari* sets appear never to exceed approximately six metres wide and about the same from front to back.[22] The studio did, however, apparently provide the facility of an understage space, which is used effectively in the fairground set: the approach to the fairground is up an inclined path which disappears behind the hillock on which the fairground (a 'meadow' in the original script) seems to stand.

Jane is brought home after being rescued. Franzis (Friedrich Feher) kneels at left

Caligari fumes as he is kept waiting by the Town Clerk

Jane, Alan (Hans-Heinz von Twardowski) and Franzis take leave of each other after visiting
Caligari's show

Cesare prepares to enter Jane's bedroom

Limitations of space clearly precluded the procession of gypsy caravans, Jane's carriage, the chase in horse-cabs – even Caligari's barrow – which Janowitz and Mayer, no doubt anticipating location shooting, had ambitiously written into the script. The finished *Caligari* is strictly a pedestrian zone.

Mayer and Janowitz's directions for the fairground, too, 'with roundabouts, barrel organ, side-show barkers, performers, wrestlers, menageries', are impractical in the circumstances: instead the designers have created a suggestive setting of brilliant effect and economy. The basis of the set is the multi-purpose painted back-cloth of Holstenwall and undefined foreground cut-outs, which previously provided the setting for Caligari's first appearance. The addition of two curious revolving elements symbolic of merry-go-rounds (on close inspection they prove to be no more than small umbrella-shaped cones of painted paper or canvas) and the eccentrically costumed crowd which throngs the small space give a wholly convincing impression of carnival. The second fairground set, with Caligari's tent, is achieved entirely with simple flats. Some changes of dramatic emphasis are evidently conditioned by the design decision. The town clerk scene, for instance, necessarily assumed different emphasis amd importance with the invention of the visual device of his extravagantly high stool.

Mayer and Janowitz's scenario is set in a distinctly modern world, with telephones, telegrams and electric light. (In the script, the prologue, evidently set in the present, describes the story as having happened twenty years before, that is about 1900.) No doubt Wiene and his designers anticipated problems in making such modern technology fit in with the fantastic design, and rigorously excluded it. The finished film evades precise indications of period. Holstenwall is a mediaeval fantasy. The costume of Caligari and the men in the fairground suggest the Biedermeier period; Jane's costumes also seem to belong to a romantic age. The policemen wear a strange, invented uniform. Cesare is quite out of time. Yet Franzis, Alan, Olfen, the doctors, the landlady, and the women and children in the fairground crowds – even Caligari when he reverts to his role as hospital Director – wear perfectly ordinary costumes of 1920. Wiene and the designers may simply not have cared, or wished deliberately to create a non-period, where the writers had as deliberately anticipated a contemporary setting for their story.

Most of the dramaturgical revisions are simply tidying-up: removing superfluous titles and editing others; cutting out unnecessary linking scenes; and re-arranging scenes so as more neatly to cover time-lapses between scenes involving the same character or characters.

Other changes, however, are positive improvements to the dramaturgical sense and structure and to psychological motivation. The Town Clerk, perched up on his ridiculously high stool as a caricature of petty authority, is made much more actively offensive to Caligari in his behaviour (he is merely 'impatient' in the script), thereby more convincingly explaining the subsequent murder. The rogue (Jakob Straat in the script) serves as the kind of red herring beloved of the detective stories then in vogue in German cinema. Wiene must have recognised though that Straat's first scenes in the script, lurking suspiciously just before Alan's murder, are an overdone and too clumsy diversion of the spectator's suspicions. Equally it was clearly a judgment of taste to cut out the bulk of the cemetery scene and the banal business of the ghost of Alan.

Much more interesting, in terms of enriching the characters and their relationships, is the 'Heimweg' scene near the end of Act II, in which Franzis reveals that he and Alan, though friends, are rivals for the love of Jane. Coming so soon before Alan's death, Franzis's violent reaction to the murder intimates complex issues of guilt – the sense of a half-conscious desire to have the rival out of the way.

The two great climaxes of the film – the awakening of Cesare and the abduction of Jane – miraculously preserve their magic even today, when much of the rest has faded into antique quaintness. Both scenes are prescribed in detail by the writers, who recognised very clearly the effects they wanted. The realisation though goes far beyond the written description, and is achieved only through the extraordinarily sympathetic interpretation, fine calculation and above all total collaboration between Wiene, the designers and the actors. Dominating all is the performance of the androgynous and sexually fascinating Veidt – concentrating Herculean struggle into the raising of the lids that cover the unearthly glare of his eyes; gliding along the wall of Jane's house like a shadow that has lost its body; transformed from seraph to vulpine beast when Jane resists.

The Framing Story
The script confirms that Mayer and Janowitz planned from the start to enclose their story within a prologue and epilogue. Thus the framing

story used in the finished film, against which Janowitz so vehemently protested and which has remained a focus of critical controversy, was not an unjustified and extraneous imposition so much as a substitution for a device already anticipated. In purely dramatic terms, the new frame might even seem stronger and more interesting than the original, which is, to say the least, somewhat prosaic and conventional.

Janowitz, as we have seen, blamed Wiene for the new frame, though Fritz Lang much later claimed to have proposed the prologue. Lang protested however when Siegfried Kracauer wrote that the overall change to the film effected by the framing device was 'in complete harmony with what Lang had planned', and counter-claimed that he had only suggested the present opening scene, with Franzis sitting on a bench recounting his story to an older man. His intention, he said, was to prepare the audience for the Expressionist settings, which might otherwise seem too startling. Lang however is a very unreliable witness. In 1970, after Hans Feld, the former editor of *Filmkurier*, described in accurate detail the prologue of the Mayer-Janowitz script, Lang wrote[23] testily as well as mistakenly that this was 'ganz unrichtig' ('quite wrong'). No subsequent writer seems to have noticed more serious discrepancies in Lang's account:

The framing prologue: Francis and another asylum patient watch Jane

> In the fall of 1919, Erich Pommer ... offered me the script of *The Cabinet of Dr. Caligari* ... Attached to the script were cubistic – (expressionist?) – sketches for the sets by Reiman, Roehrig and Warm (as far as I can remember). As I was of the opinion that a film audience (1919?) would not understand and therefore could not accept the cubistic sets, and the whole story plays in an insane asylum, I suggested to Erich Pommer that the story should be framed by a normal prologue and epilogue scene.[24]

The flaw in this version of things is that according to Warm's recollection he called in Reimann and Röhrig and proposed the design style following a meeting with Meinert and the director Wiene. Since Wiene only took over the film after Lang had been re-assigned to *Die Spinnen*, it would have been impossible for Lang to see the 'cubistic' designs which he said prompted his proposal. Moreover, the 'whole story' only played 'in an insane asylum' after the addition of the framing story.

Lang's account must therefore be discounted: Janowitz is most likely right in attributing the new framing story to Wiene.

More significant than assigning responsibility for the new frame is assessing the effect it had upon the story. In 1941 Janowitz recalled his rage that

> our symbolic story was to be explained as being a tale told by a mentally deranged person, thus dishonoring our drama – the tragedy of a man, gone mad by the misuse of his mental powers ...[25]

Six years after Janowitz wrote this, Siegfried Kracauer, eager to harness the film to the central thesis of his book *From Caligari to Hitler*, boldly re-interpreted the writers' resentment:

> Janowitz and Mayer knew why they raged against the framing story: it perverted, if not reversed, their intrinsic intentions. While the original story exposed the madness inherent in authority, Wiene's glorified authority and convicted its antagonist of madness. A revolutionary film was thus turned into a conformist one – following the much-used pattern of declaring some normal but troublesome individual insane and sending him to a lunatic asylum. This change undoubtedly resulted not so much from

split, re-formed, disagreed, chose their terms: Kandinsky's Expressionism was 'extensive'; Pechstein's, 'intensive'. Of the original groups, Die Brücke in Dresden rejected any formal programme, while Der Blaue Reiter in Munich insisted on one. Their activities were not limited to the visual arts. There was an expressionist literature and drama, and Kokoschka, Kubin, Meidner, Barlach, and Gütersloh were among the painters and sculptors who also wrote poetry, stories and plays.

The artists of Expressionism were, it is true, united by certain seminal influences and certain socio-philosophical aims. In painting, the roots of the new spirit in art were to be found in Van Gogh, Gauguin and Munch, and the discovery of El Greco and African art. Subjectivity – the compulsion to combine life and art – was an ideal, and the emphasis on egocentricity further militated against the growth of schools and styles in the narrow sense. Van Gogh and Gauguin were admired because they had made life and art all one: an artist like Munch, too, 'made his biography and psychology the theme and the object of his art'.[31] In philosophy the masters were Nietzsche, Schopenhauer, Bergson.

The term 'Expressionismus' was first chosen in deliberate opposition to 'Impressionismus'. In 1909 the manifesto of the Neue Kunstlervereinigung (New Artists' Alliance), whose president was Wassily Kandinsky, declared:

> We start from the idea that the artist, beyond the impressions which he receives from the exterior world, from nature, continually accumulates experience in his inner world, and is in quest of artistic forms which must be liberated from all irrelevant elements, so as to express only the necessary …

Philosophically the Expressionists were inspired by progress and a vision of the future. They sought to reject the materialism of the 19th century and to arrive, as the Blaue Reiter programme declared, at 'a new era of spirituality and the soul'. While earlier art historians saw the movement as coming to an end with the outbreak of the First World War and the dissolution of Die Brücke and Der Blaue Reiter, more recent scholarship views the War rather as a watershed between two distinct generations of Expressionists. The pre-war artists were imbued with spiritual and social ideals, but

The second generation suffered from war-induced disillusionment and were dissatisfied with post-war German society; they joined in with the cry for a new, classless society. They saw the war as a liberating force that had purged the old era and set the stage for a new one in which artists would be prophets.[32]

Particularly when the term is applied to the theatre and cinema, however, there is semantic confusion about the word Expressionism, succinctly analysed by John Willett;[33] the term, he explains, has varying meanings which

differ according to the context (and to some extent the country) in which they are used. Expressionism then is normally:

1. a family characteristic of modern German art, literature, music and theatre, from the turn of the century to the present day;
2. a particular modern German movement which lasted roughly between 1910 and 1922;
3. a quality of expressive emphasis and distortion which may be found in works of art of any people or period.

Willett distinguishes the second meaning by spelling it with a capital 'e'. In *Caligari* and the subsequent films it inspired – just as in the Expressionist stage productions of the years immediately following the First World War – Expressionism and expressionism (of Willett's third kind) are frequently fused and confused.

The design of *Caligari* clearly found its inspiration in theatrical precedents rather than in the more fundamental aesthetic and philosophical roots of the plastic arts of Expressionism. The writers that most typify an

Willy Hameister, *Caligari's* cameraman (Stiftung Deutsche Kinemathek)

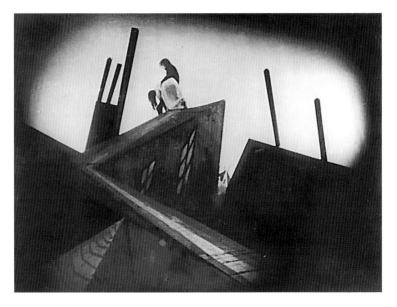

Cesare carries Jane over the rooftops

Design by Walter Reimann for the same scene

Expressionist theatre are Georg Kaiser, Ernst Toller, Walter Hasenclever,
Karl Sternheim, Fritz von Unruh and Reinhard Goering. Expressionist
drama demanded expressionist *mise en scène*. The months immediately
preceding the production of *Caligari* saw an outbreak of notable
Expressionist stagings: in Berlin, Reinhardt's productions of
Hasenclever's *Der Sohn* (1918)[34] and of Kaiser's *Von Morgen bis
Mitternachts* (January 1919), Heinrich George's production of Kaiser's
Hölle, Weg, Erde, and the presentation of Ernst Toller's first play
Die Wandlung at the short-lived Theater Der Tribüne; in Mannheim,
Weichert's production of *Der Sohn*, designed by Ludwig Siewert.
Comparison of designs and photographs from these productions with
the images of *Caligari* suggests that the film's designers had studied
these stage productions in arriving at the 'Expressionist' style of their
decors.

   Was the public of 1920 as unprepared for the novel images of
Caligari as later recollections (Lang's, for instance) assert? It seems
unlikely. By 1920 Expressionism had passed from dangerous avant-garde
to being fashionable. In 1919 Kasimir Edschmid complained that
Expressionism 'today affords titillation and edification to clergymen's
daughters and factory-owners' wives ... What once seemed a daring
gesture has now become routine. The thrust forward of the day before

Design by Ludwig Sievert for a stage production of *Penthesilea*, Frankfurt, 1920

yesterday has become the gimmick of yesterday and the big yawn of today.'[35] The work of the Expressionist artists and scenes from Expressionist stage productions were familiar from the illustrated magazines. Expressionism had gone into the streets. During the revolution period, the public had grown familiar with the propaganda posters of Max Pechstein, Heinz Fuchs, César Klein and the future avant-garde film-maker Hans Richter. More significantly, since 1918 Berlin cinemas and notably the Marmorhaus, where Caligari would have its world première, had made extensive use of the expressionist-style graphics of Josef Fenneker, whose work was so popular that he supplied more than one hundred film posters between 1919 and 1920 alone. An even more striking illustration of popular fascination with modish modern art styles was the redecoration about this time of Berlin's Luna Park in an Expressionist manner that gave the popular carnival a striking resemblance to *Caligari's* Holstenwall. Far from being a strange, frightening challenge for the public, then, Expressionism seems to have offered a positive attraction at the moment when Meinert and Wiene adopted the proposal of Warm, Reimann and Röhrig to do *Caligari* 'in Expressionist style'.

This phrase occurs often enough – in Warm's account for instance – to prompt the question whether *Caligari* is a truly and essentially Expressionist manifestation or represents only a modish pastiche applied to a conventional story. Generations of writers have passed on the vague phrase that Reimann and Röhrig were painters 'connected with the Sturm group'; but extensive research[36] has failed to discover any contribution by either artist to the exhibitions or the publications of the Sturm group. No doubt as young easel painters they must have been influenced by the currents of the time: Reimann's 'card' in a 1920 film industry yearbook[37] is illustrated with a photograph showing him in his studio, surrounded by paintings that suggest the influence of Conrad Felixmüller (who exhibited in the 1919 Novembergruppe exhibition in Berlin).

Janowitz himself (who as we have seen may well originally have been out of sympathy with the Expressionist style) asked: 'Was this particular style of painting only a garment in which to dress the drama? Was it only an accident? Would it not have been possible to change this garment, without injury to the deep effect of the drama? I do not know. But, should I be questioned today regarding the choice of style of garments, I would still maintain the style of Kubin, with his atmosphere of unreality, as that proper for this drama.'

The critics and public of the 1920s had no doubt that *Das Cabinet des Dr. Caligari* was an authentic manifestation of Expressionism, the momentous extension of the new art to a new medium. In the broader perspectives of history – and especially with the new insights provided by the Mayer–Janowitz script – we are more likely to conclude today that the Expressionist style was indeed 'only a garment in which to dress the drama'. There is no inherent Expressionist content in the original scenario. The story might equally have been handled in the naturalistic style of the popular detective stories of the time. The tormented lines and angles and crazily leaning structures, already familiar to the public from poster hoardings and outré new textile designs, were applied as a decoration – rather in the way that the same artists, only a few weeks before, had painstakingly decorated *Die Pest im Florenz* in the manner of the Italian quattrocento.

There is nothing discreditable about this; and even if the Expressionism with a large 'e' now looks like pastiche, décor, costume and performance are undeniably expressionist, with a small 'e', deriving sound lessons from current theatre practice. A set like Straat's prison cell exemplifies Willett's 'quality of expressive emphasis and distortion'. In

Caligari draws the audience

Kracauer's happy phrase, 'the settings amounted to a perfect transformation of material objects into emotional ornaments'.

Expressionist Acting

A complaint frequently voiced by critics of the time, and recurrent in subsequent discussions of *Das Cabinet des Dr. Caligari*, is the inconsistency between the stylised setting and the 'naturalism' of some of the actors. The main actors were keenly conscious of the need to adapt style and appearance to the visual character of the film. Werner Krauss and Conrad Veidt had in fact appeared on stage together in the winter of 1918 in an Expressionist drama, Reinhold Goering's *Seeschlacht*, directed at the Deutsches Theater by Max Reinhardt, and with Paul Wegener and Emil Jannings also in the cast. Krauss remembered arriving for his first day of shooting on *Caligari*:

> Conrad Veidt and myself and Dagover ... We actors got together and said 'We have to use quite different make-up. Look at the settings. Conny, you make yourself a broad line under each eye.' I disguised my nose and hair. There was a shop in the city, in a cellar,

Flashback to Caligari's hallucination: 'Du musst Caligari werden!'

where they sold old clothes. 'I need a Havelock and a top-hat and a stick with an ivory handle, all very old-fashioned, and a cape'; and an assistant director got the things, all without any artistic advice. Thus the film was played …[38]

Some of the minor roles too are very deliberately directed in a style influenced by Expressionist theatre – the town clerk on his high stool, the two policemen who sit facing each other at their desk and always move with exaggerated symmetry, the two servants who equally, sleep, wake and rise from their beds in perfect synchronisation.

Looking carefully at the other performances, particularly those of Friedrich Feher as Franzis and Hans-Heinz von Twardowski as Alan, it is tempting to suspect that the complaint centred more on the naturalistic clothing than the performances. Twardowski's strange, tormented face and Feher's large angular movements – most evident in the scene where he searches the deserted nocturnal fairground – seem to accord very passably with the writer Paul Kornfeld's definition of the task of the Expressionist actor who

> must liberate himself from reality and be merely the representative of ideas, emotions and Fate. If he has to die on the stage he should not learn to die by going to a hospital, and if he has to play the part of a drunken man he must not visit a public house to see how it is done. He should dare to spread out his arms and at a particularly inspired passage speak out as he would never speak in real life … he should not be ashamed to act, he should not disavow the theatre.[39]

This definition might apply not just to significant performances in *Caligari*, but to much of silent film acting in general.

3

. . . .

'CALIGARI' IN ITS TIME

German Film Business in 1920

Das Cabinet des Dr. Caligari arrived just when the German film industry needed it. In pre-war years German cinema had in general lagged behind the rest of Europe, and theatres depended largely on films imported from

France, Italy, America and Denmark. The war, however, cut off these markets – all film imports except from Denmark were officially banned early in 1916 – at precisely the time when demand for films escalated dramatically. With the resulting boom in domestic film production the number of production companies grew from 30 in 1913 to 250 in 1919.[40]

The authorities – recognising both the importance of films for purposes of morale and propaganda, and the threat from anti-German films shown abroad – encouraged industrial organisation. In 1917, on the initiative of General Ludendorff, the main film companies merged under an umbrella organisation, Ufa (Universum Film A.G.), with one-third of its capital provided by the state and the aim of raising standards of production and marketing.

With Germany's defeat in November 1918, control of Ufa passed to the Deutsches Bank. The tasks now were to win a place for German films in the world market, and to project a renewed and flattering image to efface that of a defeated and detested country. Film-makers explored different paths. Between the post-war suspension of censorship and the resumption of controls with the Reich Film Act of 29 May 1920, there was a brief flood of sex and 'social problem' films (Aufklärungs Filme). Detective series, which had already begun to capture the public imagination just before the war, enjoyed a new boom. Ufa saw its best chance to capture the overseas market though with the 'Kolossal' film. The pattern for massive historical and costume films was set by Joe May's *Veritas Vincit* (1918), but the most successful exponent of the genre was the former comedian Ernst Lubitsch, beginning in 1918 with two vehicles for the Polish star Pola Negri, *Die Augen der Mumie Ma* and *Carmen*. In 1919, along with a pair of frothy comedies *Die Puppe* and *Die Austernprinzessin*, Lubitsch made his most successful historical biopic in 'Kolossal' style, *Madame Dubarry*. These spectacular productions were directly influenced by Max Reinhardt's stage work, with its innovative handling of crowds and light. The 'Kolossal' films moreover were beneficiaries of Germany's precarious post-war economic situation: unemployment meant that vast crowds of extras came cheap, while a weak currency made film prices keenly competitive overseas.

Yet until the 1920s the major foreign markets remained firmly closed to all this product. Commercial suspicion and envy were added to vindictive post-war resentments. Germany's ban on imports still remained, while the film industries of the former allies watched with dismay as exports of German films to the countries of Eastern Europe boomed, raising fears of a similar westward flood of cheap but attractive German films. British exhibitors voted a five-year ban on the import of German films and equipment, while their French counterparts decided on a fifteen-year ban. The American film industry imposed no such formal sanctions, but outcry against the looming threat of cheap German film imports grew louder.

From May 1920 the Reich Film Act permitted the import of foreign films up to 15% of the number of films shown in German cinemas. This gesture, modest as it was, reopened relations with foreign film industries. *Caligari* was one of the earliest films to benefit.

Along with Lubitsch's 'Kolossal' films, *Caligari* inaugurated a novel commercial film export: Art – new, exciting, and above all both visible and fashionable. The year after the American release of *Caligari*, the American actor and humorist Will Rogers inserted a title in his film *The Ropin' Fool*: 'If you think this picture's no good, I'll put on a beard and say it was made in Germany. Then you'll call it art.'

Impact of 'Caligari'

Viewing *Das Cabinet des Dr. Caligari* and similar 'classic' films today, we are faced with the problem that with time they have become segregated, to form the special class of 'art' films, viewed as something separate from the main line of industrial production. A scholar even of the historical sensitivity of Thomas Elsaesser considers that German Expressionist cinema must be discussed

> in the context of a self-conscious attempt to make 'art' in the cinema and to appeal to a specific, self-selected part of the audience ... The latter, of course, applies with especial force to a film like *The Cabinet of Dr. Caligari*, conceived and marketed very deliberately as a highbrow product ...[41]

On the contrary, to see *Caligari* in proper historical perspective we have to recognise that it was made, knowingly and strategically, in the main line of the commercial production of its day, with the 'art' element calculated as an extra and positive, if speculative box-office attraction.

In 1920 there was no separate 'art cinema' in the sense of something elitist and esoteric. Louis Delluc and the first avant-garde

4 4   Design for a poster (Stiftung Deutsche Kinemathek)

were just girding up in Paris, Viking Eggeling and Hans Richter were making their abstract films in Berlin, and just before the Revolution the Russian futurists had made some playful motion picture essays; but even they expected their films to be shown in ordinary cinemas and liked – or not liked, as the case might be – by regular audiences. Conscious and deliberate efforts to introduce 'art' content into film, like the pre-World War One 'Films d'Art' in France, 'Famous Players in Famous Plays' in America and the 'Autorenfilm' in Germany were not a result of some altruistic mission to elevate the medium and to educate its patrons. At the end of the first decade of the century the cinema's great strength was that it remained above all a popular and proletarian entertainment, catering for the masses in fairgrounds and nickelodeons. Smart entrepreneurs like Pathé, Zukor or Messter nevertheless recognised that there was a vast additional public to be won if the prejudices of the middle class could be overcome. One strategy was to build new cinemas that compared in size and splendour with the grandest legitimate theatres. Another was to offer the reassurance and the lure of Art. It is important to recognise that the idea behind such moves was to enlarge the audience, not to change or to restrict it. So the Art content had to be presented and marketed in a way that would continue to be attractive to the mass audience, while drawing in the more discerning patron.

When the Decla management approved *Caligari* for production, they certainly had not a minority or exclusive audience in view. Erich Pommer recalled of his first meeting with Mayer and Janowitz:

> While they talked about art, I was thinking of quite a different aspect of the script. The mysterious and macabre atmosphere of Grand Guignol was in vogue in German films at that time, and this film fitted the taste exactly. They saw in the script an 'Experiment' – I saw a relatively cheap film.

Meinert, as we have seen, told the designers to do the sets 'as eccentrically as you are able', because he confidently calculated that the 'crazy design' would ensure the film's 'success as a sensation, regardless of whether the press turned out negative or positive'. He foresaw the outré visual style not as a turn-off but as a positive bait for the public. Expressionism was in the air and in fashion. It was foreseeable that the public would be titillated and flattered by the painless and spectacular participation in the new visual excitement that *Caligari* offered – and there was always the fall-back that the strange distorted images could be explained away as the fantasies of a diseased mind.

. . . .

Das Cabinet des Dr. Caligari had its world première at the Marmorhaus, Berlin on 26 February 1920. The most absurd and readily disprovable story in the mass of legend surrounding the film is that it was a failure on its first appearance. This fantasy seems entirely attributable to the unreliable Pommer, always eager to build a heroic role for himself in the *Caligari* story. He told George Huaco in the 1950s:[42] '*Caligari* opened in a Berlin theater, but the audience demonstrated against it and asked for its money back, so after two performances the theater threw it out; and I couldn't get another theater to show the film.' After this set-back, Pommer claimed, he spent six months on a publicity campaign and finally re-launched *Caligari* at his own risk, whereupon it ran successfully for three months at the theatre where it had first been shown.

Manvell and Fränkel[43] assert that the film

> was shelved after its completion for lack of a suitable outlet. It achieved its screening at the Marmorhaus (Marble House) in Berlin only through an accident, when another film had fallen through.

This again is absurd: not only was the film premièred less than one month after its completion, but the Marmorhaus was the most prestigious theatre in the Kurfurstendamm: films did not arrive on the screen there through 'accidents'. On the contrary the marketing and exhibition of *Das Cabinet des Dr. Caligari* were evidently planned with great care. The film's release was heralded by an inventive advertising campaign, focussing on the enigmatic slogan that exhorted, 'Du musst Caligari werden!' ('You must become Caligari!'), and which began to appear on posters and in newspaper advertisements even before the film was completed. The musical accompaniment for the première run was compiled by Giuseppe Becce (1877–1973), the most gifted and prolific composer for silent films. The score does not exist, though a number of the themes are included in Becce's great anthology of music for silent film accompaniment, the 12-volume *Kinethek* (1919–1933).

Janowitz recalled the nervy journey from the Decla offices in Friedrichstrasse to the première. Riding in the same car with Mayer, Pommer and Pommer's assistant Sternheim, the writers were still fuming over their resentment against the framing story, and few words were exchanged until Pommer blurted out what all were thinking: 'It will be a horrible failure for all of us!'

In the outcome, the audience were spellbound. A woman screamed out at the moment when Cesare's eyes open. Several (at least according to Janowitz) fainted, groaned or shrieked when Cesare abducted the sleeping Jane. Janowitz recorded that:

When the picture ended, there was a stunned silence. Mayer and I, standing at the back of the gallery, looked at each other. So it had been a failure? Suddenly this stunned silence was shattered by applause, applause rising to a crescendo that broke into a thunderous outburst of frantic calling and clapping, a raving audience, shouting with joy and acclamation. Again we looked at each other: 'Well! It's a success!'.

Robert Wiene, Erich Pommer, the actors, painters, and photographers acknowledged the applause. Not we, the authors. We beat a hasty retreat to a nearby liqueur-buffet, drank Mampe, half-and-half, considered our future, and wondered whether our future scripts would also be produced in a crippled form by cowardly directors.

The German critics, almost without exception, ranged from favourable to ecstatic. Despite a few days' interruption caused by a general strike, the film remained at the Marmorhaus for a then exceptional four weeks; and was brought back two weeks later. In its seventh week the newspaper advertisements still proclaimed 'Täglich ausverkauft' ('Sold Out Every Day'). Following the Marmorhaus run *Caligari* seems to have remained for months in the Berlin film repertory while enjoying a nation-wide release.

The film was acquired for American distribution by the Goldwyn company. The New York première took place on 3 April 1921 at the huge and splendid Capitol Cinema at 51st street and Broadway, at that time run by the master showman Samuel F. ('Roxy') Rothafel. In the fashion of the time, for the première run the film was given a live prologue and epilogue, which provided an extra frame to the narrative. In the stage prologue a character identified as 'Cranford' introduced the first scene, representing himself as the gentleman to whom Franzis, in the opening sequence of the film, is telling his story. In the epilogue, 'Cranford' conveys the happy news that Franzis is today fully recovered. For a modern critic, Mike Budd,

> It is difficult to imagine a more blatant attempt to force a problematic text into conventional form, to contain its excesses in a frame of authoritarian and commodifying realism.[44]

Perhaps this is reading too much into what would have seemed at the time a perfectly normal piece of theatrical presentation for a first-run, big-city theatre. The *New York Times* merely noted that the prologue and epilogue were 'calculated to supply an atmosphere of usualness and a happy ending for those who demand them'.[45]

There is a danger, too, of over-estimating the extent to which *Caligari* was, in Budd's phrase, a 'problematic text' for the American audience of 1921 any more than for the German public. In its review the trade magazine *Variety*, whose function was to try to anticipate the reaction of the popular audience, concluded that this was

> a mystery story told in the Poe manner and fairly prods the interest along at a high pace. Of first importance is the direction and cutting. This has resulted in a series of actions so perfectly dovetailed as to carry the story through at a perfect tempo. Robert Wiene has made perfect use of settings designed by Hermann Warm, Walter Reimann and Walter Roehrig, settings that squeeze and turn and adjust the eye and through the eye the mentality.

Like the German public, Americans were already exposed to the styles of modernist art: it was already eight years since the popular press had made a field day of the historic Armory show. Indeed the *New York Times* review of *Caligari* recalled the most publicised work from that exhibition: 'Its settings bear a somewhat closer resemblance to reality than, say, the famous "Nude Descending a Staircase" [by Marcel Duchamp].'

Far from softening the impact for his audiences, Rothafel compounded it by collaborating with the Hungarian-born musical director Ernö Rapee to compile an appropriate accompaniment from challenging new music – Strauss, Schönberg, Debussy, Stravinsky, Prokofiev. 'A film conceived along revolutionary lines', declared Rothafel,

> called for a score faithfully sychronised in mood and development ... The music had, as it were, to be made eligible for citizenship in a nightmare country.

The musical practices of cinema theatres, with accompaniments often compiled from the works of the most heterogeneous composers, can easily shock modern sensibilities. Mike Budd sees the Rothafel-Rapee score as a further stage in standardization and commodification:

> Associating it with distortion, nightmares, and insanity, they took modernist music out of the history of music and dropped it, in decontextualized fragments and motifs, into another system of interchangeable parts.[46]

We must recognise though the part music in cinemas played in the education of a popular public before the days of radio and sophisticated recording techniques. A music critic of the time, Bernard Rogers, writing in *Musical America* exulted that:

> Properly, the American première of *Caligari* employed music calculated to heighten its exotic character, to underline its fantastic aspects ... As briefly back as five years Stravinsky or Schönberg in the movie-house belonged to the inconceivable. Today it calmly happens, and the audience calmly swallows the pill. It would have been far simpler in preparing acompaniment for this film, to dish up the old safe and sickening potpourri. The more admirable, then, is the departure made by Messrs Rothafel and Rappee. The thing took more than courage; it meant double labor and it meant considerable expense. Four rehearsals were called.[47] But the tune was worth the toll. The acrid air of Stravinsky has been borne into the film theater. It may clear the sweet murk before the last reel is run.[48]

The American press was by and large as enthusiastic as the German critics, confirming *Variety*'s untroubled acceptance of the novel visual qualities. The *New York Times* said that

> the story is coherent, logical, a genuine and legitimate thriller, and after one has followed it through several scenes the weird settings seem to be of its substance and no longer call disturbing attention to themselves.[49]

Many American critics followed *Variety* in styling the story, reassuringly, as 'Poe-like' (*Motion Picture News*: 'It is like a page from Poe'; *New York Times*: 'a fantastic story of murder and madness such as Edgar Allan Poe might have written').

Generally it was agreed that *Caligari* was Art, indicating new possibilities, vistas, and hoped-for aspirations for the movies. In *Motion Picture Classic* a 27-year-old critic, Albert Lewin – later a Hollywood writer-producer of self-consciously artistic inclination and the director of *The Picture of Dorian Gray* and *Pandora and the Flying Dutchman* – hailed it as

> the only serious picture, exhibited in America so far, that in anything like the same degree has the authentic thrills and shock of art. The tale of a madman unfolded thru mad scenery by mad characters has greater intrinsic reality than any of our flat photographic pictures. It ceases to be merely a succession of photographs, and becomes alive – a creation, spiritually real and vital in a way peculiar to the screen, as unthinkable in any other form as are the poems of Heine.
>
> This expressive explosivenesss – this dynamic reality – has been achieved in pictures only by Chaplin and the creators of Caligari … Charlie Chaplin and *The Cabinet of Dr. Caligari*, in divergent and equally convincing ways, have established beyond cavil the integrity of the motion picture as an art. There is no longer any need for doubt or discouragement.

Since box-office figures were not regularly published at that period, it is harder to assess the commercial performance of *Caligari* in the United States. Two American researchers, Kristin Thompson and David B.

Pratt[50] have diligently combed the trade press of the period and daringly extrapolated from the evidence they discovered there – only to arrive at contrary conclusions about the comparative success (Thompson) or failure (Pratt) of *Caligari*. Their accounts do however coincide in suggesting that *Caligari*, along with other German films which arrived in the United States at about the same time, established a pattern which has persisted for imported European films in which critics and public identify an 'art' content. Enthusiastic business in New York and the major cities is rarely matched by box office performance in smaller centres where taste is more conservative.

In the building of the Caligari legend, much has been made of the circumstances of the Los Angeles première, at Miller's Theater on 7 May 1921, when demonstrators forced the management to take off the film. It is clear however that this had nothing to do with aesthetic objections to the film or even with generalised anti-German sentiments. The protest was organised by the Hollywood branch of the American Legion as part of a protest raised in fear of the spectre of mass unemployment as a result of a (wholly imaginary) imminent flood of German films into America.[51]

The French film industry shared this anxiety about the threat of German film importations. On 14 November 1921, however, Louis Delluc engineered a single screening of *Caligari* in the course of a benefit performance in aid of the Spanish Red Cross at the Colisée cinema in Paris. Shortly afterwards the Cosmograph company were emboldened to buy the film, which opened at the Ciné-Opéra on 3 March 1922. Prejudice was conquered by the film's instant critical and popular success, even if the press was not unanimous. The most famous hostile commentary was that of Blaise Cendrars, writing in Delluc's own magazine, *Cinéa*, 2 June 1922. Generally only selectively cited, Cendrars' review is worth reprinting in full, since it so neatly summarises practically all the criticisms that were to be levelled at the film at various times in the subsequent three quarters of a century:[52]

COMMENT
The Cabinet of Dr. Caligari
I don't like this film. Why?
Because it is a film of misapprehension.
Because it is a film that casts discredit on all modern Art.
Because it is hybrid, hysterical, unwholesome.

Because it is not cinema.

Film of misapprehension because it is faked and dishonest.

Casts discredit on modern Art because the discipline of modern painters (Cubist) is not the hyper sensibility of madmen but equilibrium, intensity and mental geometry.

Hybrid, hysterical, unwholesome because it is hybrid, hysterical, unwholesome (vive the cowboys!)

It is not cinema because

1. The pictorial deformations are only tricks (new modern conventions);
2. Real characters in unreal sets;
3. The deformations are not optical and do not depend on the angle of taking, nor on the objective, nor on the lens, nor on the focus;
4. There is never any unity;
5. Theatrical;
6. Movement, but no rhythm;
7. No purification of the technique, all the effects obtained by the aid of means belonging to painting, music, literature, etc.

ONE IS NEVER AWARE OF THE CAMERA

8. Sentimental and not visual;
9. Good photography, good lighting, superexcellent;
10. Good business.

French film-makers were divided. Abel Gance for one was inspired: 'The film is superb! What a lesson to all directors!' Others were violently critical, among them Jean Epstein:

> If you have to say that a film has fine décors, I think it is better not to speak of it at all: the film is bad. *The Cabinet of Dr. Caligari* is the prize example of the abuse of décor in the cinema. Caligari represents a grave sickness of cinema ... Everything in Caligari is décor, the décor itself first of all, then the actor who is painted and tricked out like the décor, finally the light – unpardonable sacrilege in the cinema! – which is also painted, with lights and shadows mendaciously distributed in advance. So the film is nothing but a still life, all the living elements killed by a brush ...[53]

Jean Cocteau, who a decade later would consider playing the role of
Cesare in a remake of the film by Robert Wiene, also thought the film

> the first step towards a grave error which consists of flat
> photography of eccentric décors, instead of obtaining surprise by
> means of the camera.[54]

4

....

THE 'CALIGARI' LEGACY

Influence

The era of German Expressionist cinema began with *Caligari*.

In the immediate wake of the film, a handful of films attempted to
emulate its stylised Expressionist design. Wiene himself failed to repeat
his success with *Genuine* (1920) which suffered from a stupid melodrama
story and muddly sets that did less than credit to its designer, César
Klein, an eminent Expressionist, known for his paintings, posters and
stage designs. Wiene had better luck with *Raskolnikov* (1923), given a
more substantial scenario and a designer, Andrei Andreiev, who though
not personally committed to Expressionism, understood better how to
use its conventions within the film frame. Andreiev later used the
Expressionist experience to effect in G.W. Pabst's *Die Buchse der
Pandora* (1928) and *Dreigroschenoper* (1931). Hanns Kobe's *Torgus*
(1921), which Lotte Eisner describes as 'a rather poor film' no longer
survives, though stills indicate the use of a purely decorative
'Expressionist' style. *Von Morgens bis Mitternachts*, made in the same
year as *Caligari*, is a unique instance of a film directly based on
an Expressionist stage play, by Georg Kaiser. The director
Karlheinz Martin came from the theatre to make his screen debut
with this film, though neither he nor the designer Robert Neppach
seems to have worked on previous stage productions of the piece. A
second Martin-Neppach collaboration, also apparently in Expressionist
style, *Das Haus ʒum Mond* (1921) has unfortunately not survived. Nor is
there today any trace of an Expressionist experiment, *Das haus ohne
Türen und Fenster* (1921), scripted by Thea von Harbou (the wife of Fritz
Lang) and directed by Friedrich Feher, the actor who plays Franzi
in *Caligari*.

If no subsequent film was to commit itself so fully to the formal character of the style, the essence of expressionism as distinct from Expressionism – the use of setting, design, lighting and chiaroscuro to reflect and express the psychology of the characters – was to persist in German cinema of the 1920s.

One immediate effect of *Caligari* upon German film practice of the 1920s was to drive production into the studios and away from location shooting. For several years most major German feature films were 100% studio made: the entire forest of Lang's *Nibelungen* (1923–4), for instance, was built on the stages of Babelsberg. The effect of this was to give supreme importance in German studios to the designer – or 'architect', in German studio usage.

The later silent period witnessed a remarkable generation of these designer-architects, who included – besides Warm, Reimann and Röhrig – Robert Herlth, Hans Dreier, Rochus Gliese, Paul Leni, Ernö Metzner, Rudolph Bamberger, Erich Kettelhut, Otto Hunte, Karl Vollbrecht, Albin Grau, Ludwig Meidner, Hans Poelzig, Alfred Junge and Otto Erdmann. The successive waves of emigration that resulted in turn from Hollywood's eager recruitment of European talent and from Nazi persecution, scattered many of these talents and their influence abroad. British film design was invigorated by the arrival of Alfred Junge. The distinctive Paramount look was due almost solely to the influence of Hans Dreier, one of the first emigrés. The apotheosis of expressionism was Rochus Gliese's design of Friedrich Wilhelm Murnau's Hollywood production *Sunrise* (1927). In its most developed visual styles, the American *film noir* of the forties and fifties reveals the legacy of German Expressionism as clearly as the American musical shows the pervading influence of Austro-Hungarian operetta.

Critical history

When the Exposition Universelle et Internationale held in Brussels in 1958 organised a poll of 120 international film critics to decide on the best films of all time, *Das Cabinet des Dr. Caligari* stood at twelfth place. Four years later, when *Sight and Sound* organised the second of its decennial polls, *Caligari* did not make the list of finalists. In the 1992 *Sight and Sound* poll, the film found only a single vote (from the South Korean director Park Kwang-su) among the 230 critics and film-makers who responded.

This is an ignominious fall from the peak of the film's reputation, when Paul Rotha, in his pioneering history *The Film Till Now* (1930) could write that *Das Cabinet des Dr. Caligari* stood with *The Battleship Potemkin*

> as the two most momentous advances in the development of the cinema till now ...
>
> It was, once and for all, the first attempt at the expression of a creative mind in the new medium of cinematography. In ten years the film has risen to the greatest heights, as fresh now as when first produced, a masterpiece of dramatic form and content ... *The Cabinet of Dr. Caligari* put forward these dominating facts, which have lain at the back of every intelligent director's mind to this day: that, for the first time in the history of the cinema, the director has worked *through* the camera and broken with realism on the screen; that a film could be effective dramatically when not photographic; and finally, of the greatest possible importance, that the mind of the audience was brought into play psychologically.
>
> As a film, *The Cabinet of Dr. Caligari* asked everything of its audience. They were to take part and believe in the wild imaginings of a madman. They were to share his distorted idea of the professor of the lunatic asylum in which he (the lunatic) and they (the audience) were confined. The theme and conception were absolutely remarkable ... *The Cabinet of Dr. Caligari* served to attract to the cinema audience many people who had hitherto regarded the film as the low watermark of intelligence.[55]

Rotha's strictly aesthetic valuation was to characterise all writing on *Caligari* before 1947. A decade after Rotha, the American historian Lewis Jacobs called it

> revelatory and challenging ... Its stylized rendition, brooding quality, lack of explanation, and distorted settings were new to the film world.[56]

We have already seen that, despite their left-wing sympathies and developed political sensitivity, neither Rotha nor Jacobs – any more than the rest of their contemporaries – sought or found any symbolic political meaning in the film. Attitudes to *Caligari* changed dramatically after 1947 and the appearance of Siegfried Kracauer's book *From Caligari to Hitler*. Kracauer (1889–1966), a historian, sociologist and former Berlin journalist, emigrated to New York in 1941. After two years working at the Museum of Modern Art, he was awarded a Guggenheim Fellowship to write a history of the German cinema. At that time, with film histories of any kind thin on the ground, Kracauer's proposition, that films could reflect the inner dispositions and collective psychology of an entire nation, was novel, gripping and attractive. Its impact and influence on film criticism and historiography have persisted, even though the extent to which Kracauer was obliged to bend both the history of the nation and the history of its cinema to suit his thesis has become more apparent with subsequent study of German cinema. As the title of his book indicates, *Das Cabinet des Dr. Caligari* was Kracauer's foundation stone; and Decla's novelty horror film was made to carry a massive weight of significance:

> The character of Caligari ... stands for an unlimited authority that idolizes power as such, and, to satisfy its lust for domination, ruthlessly violates all human rights and values. Functioning as a mere instrument, Cesare is not so much a guilty murderer as Caligari's innocent victim ...
>
> Whether intentionally or not, *Caligari* exposes the soul wavering between tyranny and chaos and facing a desperate situation: any escape from tyranny seems to throw it into a state of utter confusion. Quite logically, the film spreads an all-pervading atmosphere of horror. Like the Nazi world, that of *Caligari* overflows with sinister portents, acts of terror and outbursts of panic.

Kracauer's view of *Caligari* as a reflection of the dark reaches of the German soul persisted. Some redress was provided by Lotte Eisner, adopting the approach of art historian in tracing the Expressionist impulse in German cinema. She could admire the Expressionist treatment of *Caligari* for

> evoking the 'latent physiognomy' of a small mediaeval town, with its dark, twisting back-alleys boxed in by crumbling houses whose

inclined façades keep out all daylight. Wedge-shaped doors with heavy shadows and oblique windows with distorted frames seem to gnaw into the walls. The bizarre exaltation brooding over the synthetic sets of *Caligari* bring to mind Edschmid's statement that 'Expressionism evolves in a perpetual excitation'. These houses and the well, crudely sketched at an alley-corner, do indeed seem to vibrate with an extraordinary spirituality.

More recently the ambiguities of *Caligari*'s history have made it a favourite for the kind of 'film studies' approach based upon 'using' a 'text', rather than analysing a work of cinema – drawing selectively upon the history and fabric of a film to provide partial materials to support elaborate and decorative edifices of (often bogus) theory. Better academic writing, like the essays in Professor Mike Budd's 1990 anthology *The Cabinet of Dr. Caligari: Texts, Contexts, Histories*, illuminates particular facets of the film. Budd himself approaches the film from the standpoint of Marxist economic theory, paying particular attention to the tensions (today self-evident) between the modernist visual form and the conventional narrative form – 'Expressionist elements ... bolted on to a realist narrative'. In the same volume, the feminist writers Catherine B. Clément and Patrice Petro shift their focus to the character of Jane, Clément paralleling her relationship with Caligari to that between Freud and one of his hysteric patients; Petro linking Jane and the somnambulist as forces that in part escape the male need for control. This emphasis on the role of Jane brings out an erotic element in the film ignored by earlier writers: she is first shown as the object of erotic competition between the friends Franzis and Alan. Later Caligari lures her into his tent for a portentous encounter with Cesare (giving her, as Richard J. Murphy of Columbia University unfortunately phrases it, 'a private showing of his erect somn-ambulist'[57]). The abduction of Jane, which leads to the death of Cesare represents the perennial beauty-and-the-beast theme, later parallelled in *King Kong* where also 'It was Beauty killed the Beast!'

Resurrection

The initial success and lasting fame of *Das Cabinet des Dr. Caligari* inevitably led to projects for remakes or sequels. In 1934, Robert Wiene, by this time living in exile, bought the rights from Ufa and battled both in London and in Paris to find backing for a remake in which he planned to cast Jean Cocteau in the role of Cesare. The French script – unsigned but most likely by Wiene himself – indicates that the new film would have been modernised to the extent of supplanting the expressionist style of 1920 with a currently modish surrealist look.

In American exile, both Pommer and Janowitz endeavoured to set up remakes, and this helps explain the eagerness of both men to claim key roles in the authorship of the original film. Their struggles are witnessed by extensive files of documents now in the Stiftung Deutsche Kinemathek. The inextricable confusion over the rights following Ufa's sale of them to Wiene in 1934 and Wiene's subsequent death in 1938, were compounded by the invalidity of Nazi law in the United States, and by legal uncertainty over the relation of rights in sound and silent films.

In early 1945, Janowitz seemed close to selling his rights in a script to be directed by Fritz Lang, but neither that nor his plans for a sequel, *Caligari II* materialised. In 1947 he appears to have been involved with another German emigré, Ernst Matray, on a project titled *The Return of Caligari*, which the English director Victor Saville was eager to direct: this version would have been modernised to make Caligari a former Nazi officer.

Only after Janowitz's death were the rights extricated, for an undistinguished remake distributed by 20th Century-Fox. Directed by Roger Kay and scripted by the writer of Hitchcock's *Psycho*, Robert Bloch, the 1962 production *The Cabinet of Dr Caligari* has only tenuous connections with the original. In conventional décors, Glynis Johns plays a woman held prisoner by Dr Caligari (Dan O'Herlihy). At the end of the film it is revealed that the story has all been her delusion: Caligari is merely her psychiatrist, who ends up curing her.

Residue

What remains of *Das Cabinet des Dr. Caligari* today, now that it no longer has a place in the top ten lists, and has become a skittle for games of 'film studies'? Today few could echo the faith and enthusiasm of critics of the twenties and thirties who saw the film as a giant leap for world culture, the ultimate fusion of the infant cinema with the senior and finer arts. Yet historically this confidence served a purpose, luring an influential new public to the cinema and focussing more serious attention on the potential of the medium. Nor is Kracauer's view of the film as a pregnant metaphor of the German psyche and a portent of the nightmares to come as convincing or attractive as it appeared half a century ago.

Today we are more inclined to see *Caligari* as a vintage silent film among the rest – though one of the more attractive, deserving restoration and revival on the merits of its own attractions as well as its historical status. The mystery story, with its eerie overtones, is well enough constructed and narrated to command attention and curiosity, even to this day. The décors are still interesting and arresting in their own right and complement the mood of the story, even if we now tend to regard them, in Janowitz's phrase, as 'only a garment in which to dress the drama', which might equally well (if less effectively) have been presented in realist style. Historically, they are an invaluable document of the 'Expressionist' manner in *mise en scène* which figured briefly in German theatre practice in the post-World War One years.

Above all, *Caligari* lives on in the iconic presences created by its two main actors, Krauss's grotesque and grimacing Caligari, and Veidt's magical black-clad wraith with hypnotic eyes, the somnambulist Cesare. However accidental the circumstances that made them, they have left their indelible trace in the century's mythology.

APPENDIX: THE TWO 'CALIGARIS' – A COMPARISON OF THE SCENARIO AND THE COMPLETED FILM

. . . .

The division of the film (and script) into 'Acts' was customary in German films throughout the 1920s: the convention appears to have been less a legacy from the theatre than a hangover from the period, just before the First World War, when the one-reel film began to give way to the multi-reel feature. Projectionists took time to work out smooth reel-change techniques; some cinemas still had only one projector; and some distributors persisted for a while in 'serialising' multi-reel films. Film-makers therefore found it advisable to anticipate interruptions in screenings by giving each reel its own structural and dramatic integrity.

It is convenient therefore to examine the way that *Caligari* was translated from Mayer and Janowitz's 'Filmroman' to the screen, act by act. (To help distinguish the script narrative from the film narrative, the summary of the former is printed in italic, and uses the original form of character names; the latter uses the definitive versions of names as they appear in the film).

ACT ONE

Scenario

The script begins with a prologue (partially transcribed above), set on the terrace of a country house, where Francis and his wife Jane are entertaining three gentlemen and four ladies. A procession of gypsy caravans passes in the distance, beyond the park, and this occurrence produces an emotional reaction in Francis and Jane. At the request of his friends he starts to relate the circumstances of 'a dreadful tale' in which the couple were involved, more than twenty years before, when Francis was working as a private tutor in Holstenwall, 'an idyllic old small town'...

The old town is seen in the setting sun. A procession of gypsy wagons is silhouetted against 'the wide landscape'. A title explains that the procession included 'jener geheimnisvolle Mann' ('that mysterious man'): Calligaris appears, in his flowing cloak and tall hat, following the procession and stopping now and then to leaf through a big book.

In the narrow streets of the old town there are excited preparations for the fair. Allan, a young student, sees the bustle from the window of his room, goes out into the street, and calls on his friend Francis, to invite him to come to the fair.

Meanwhile in a meadow outside the city wall, the fairground is being erected. Calligaris enters the scene, chooses a plot, measures it, pegs it out and asks where he should apply for permission for his show. Some bystanders lead him to an office, where he is obliged to bribe a clerk to take him to the town clerk, Dr Lüders. Dr Lüders is annoyed and impatient since he is just about to leave his office.

A title announces 'Next day'. The fair is in full swing. Calligaris is putting the final touches to his booth, and the crowd gapes at the sign which announces, 'Der somnambule Mensch'. Calligaris inspects the work, looks at his watch and goes off through the streets.

Arriving at a caravan bearing a sign 'Dr Calligaris Cabinett' he loads a 'black, coffin-like, big box fitted with obvious locks' onto a barrow. With this he returns to the booth. The crowd watches with interest as some workmen help him to unload the box and stand it upright on the podium, 'like a cupboard'.

Calligaris unlocks the box, opens the lid and 'the astonished crowd sees a motionless standing figure in a black, tight-fitting, old-fashioned jersey-suit, its face with wide-open, expressionless eyes staring into space. Calligaris grins weirdly, then dances round the figure and pats its cheek.

A fade-out ends Act I.

The finished film diverges markedly from this narrative. Most significant – and ultimately most controversial – is the new framing prologue. The opening scene of the film is now set in a lunatic asylum. A handsome young man (Franzis) sits on a bench with an older gentleman of distinctly crazed appearance. A wraithlike young woman in

Bild: Vor dem Wagen!

14 Dr. Olfen und Francis stehen an
der Treppe, der letztere ersucht
Calligaris, der sich an der Tür
stehend an einem Tuch die
Hände reinigt, um Einlaß. Calligaris betrachtet sie mißtrauisch
und lehnt ab. Als die Beiden
dringlicher werden, und Olfens
einen Schritt nach der Tür zu
macht, verwehrt Calligaris ihm
nochmals mit heftiger Geberde
den Eintritt und steigt sehr
wütend die Treppen herunter.

Titel: Dr. Olfens stellte sich Calligaris vor
und forderte energisch den
Somnambulen zu ~~sehen~~ untersuchen
Während wir so mit Calligaris stritten
trug sich in einem anderen Teil Holsten

Facsimile page of the script (Stiftung Deutsche Kinemathek)

a white dress passes them without a glance. Franzis explains 'That is my bride' and begins his story...

'Holstenwall – the little town where I was born'. There is no longer a procession of gypsy caravans. Holstenwall is presented as a painted backdrop, varied in a second view by the addition of some foreground elements.

Franzis exclaims (in a title) 'Er ...'('Him ...'); and Caligari comes unsteadily into the shot, grimacing as his face is isolated in an iris-out.

A title 'Alan – mein Freund' introduces a sequence as described in the script: Alan, working in his room, is distracted by the noise of the fair, and goes in search of Franzis. The two walk together down the street, followed shortly afterwards by the sinister figure of Caligari.

Caligari is on his way to the office of the town clerk. As in the script he bribes the clerk to gain admission to the town clerk; but after that the sequence is much elaborated. The town clerk, perched on an absurdly high stool, rudely tells him, twice, 'Warten!' ('Wait!'). Caligari visibly fumes with anger.

From a detail of what looks like a turning merry-go-round in the top right-hand corner of the screen, the picture irises out to a view of Holstenwall. The 'merry-go-round' – in fact a small umbrella-like abstract scenic element – has simply been added to the painted background already seen; a second, smaller umbrella-'merry-go-round' twirls in the lower left-hand corner of the scene. A crowd of people in Biedermeier-style costume throngs the space. Caligari enters, peering curiously at the passers-by, who include a dwarf in a tall, conical hat.

Another part of the fairground: people pass a tent that bears no sign. Caligari emerges from the tent and unfurls a banner advertising 'Cesare the Somnambule'. Caligari draws back the tent flap and invites the public to enter. A title declares

'... Here is to be seen for the first time, Cesare the somnambulist!'.

ACT II
Scenario
An inter-title characteristic of the lengthy and often redundant explanatory titles in the script (supposed to be the words of Francis' framing narrative) tells us:

> *Next day, as we made our way to the fair, we did not suspect that in the meantime a horrible crime had been committed.*

A police commissioner and two officials are examining a bedroom whose disorder and broken window indicate that some violence has taken place. The commissioner explains (in a title) that the town clerk, Dr Lüders, has been killed by stabbing with a sharp instrument. Another title shows a handbill,

> *Murder in Holstenwall! 1000 marks reward. Last night Dr Lüders in his home ...*

Francis and Allan walk light-heartedly through the town, passing one of the officials entering the printer's shop.

The fairground is full of activity, with roundabouts, barrel organ, side-show barkers, performers, wrestlers, menageries. Francis and Allan hurry to Calligaris' booth, where he is shouting the wonders of his show. Caesare stands outside the booth, staring vacantly into space. Calligaris bows and grimaces, and the public push into the booth. Francis and Allan buy their tickets and follow.

A title announces 'Das Cabinet des Dr. Calligaris'. Inside the booth – 'a primitive, poor tent, lit with a few feeble lamps … a little curtain hangs over the improvised stage' – Calligaris rings a bell to attract the audience.

Outside the booth, a group of undecided people wander off to other shows. Among them lingers Jakob Straat, who is not described in the script, though in the cast list he is 'ein Gauner' ('a rogue'). He reads the poster and then, with indifference, enters the show.

Inside, Caesare stands on the stage, lit by a shaft of light. Calligaris orders him to wake.

CLOSE-UP CAESARE

Caesare stands motionless for a few seconds. Under the piercing gaze of Calligaris, who stands beside him, he now becomes quite tender and something like expression enters his face! His eyes blink, now quite gentle and distant. Then quietly and with great physical effort he begins again and again to gasp. With slightly opened mouth, he struggles for air. The rock-like rigidity of the body gives way to a sudden violent shaking of the limbs. The dangling arms are raised, as if automatically, in a constrained movement, reaching forward as if to embrace something. With his gradual awakening, whose climax is evidently an intense physical process, he seems to become suddenly helpless and begins to topple forwards. At this moment the grinning Calligaris catches him, and stands him up back in his place like a dummy. Caesare's face and body betray his struggle to get air.

Calligaris announces that Caesare will now answer any question and reveal the deepest secrets. Allan, clearly intrigued by the somnambulist, pushes to the stage, despite Francis' efforts to restrain him. He asks, 'How long will I live?'. Caesare stares at him, then tells him 'Until dawn'. The shocked Allan returns the somnambulist's stare, then breaks into laughter, as does Francis, who pulls his friend away from the show.

In the square, in front of the old town hall, Francis and Allan read the notice announcing the murder of Dr Lüders. Allan is strangely fascinated; but they are interrupted by the arrival of Jane in a carriage. They accompany her to her home, 'a country house in a park beside a river'.

Back in the town, Francis and Allan bid each other goodnight.

Meanwhile 'In darkest Holstenwall', Jakob Straat emerges from the shadows of 'a crumbling lane', then disappears as mysteriously as he came.

Allan enters his room, lights the lamp, opens the window and stretches out into the night air; then goes to bed. He reads, nods over the book and then turns out the light.

The remainder of the scene, one of the most intriguing sections of the script, is a manuscript addition, in two different hand-writings.

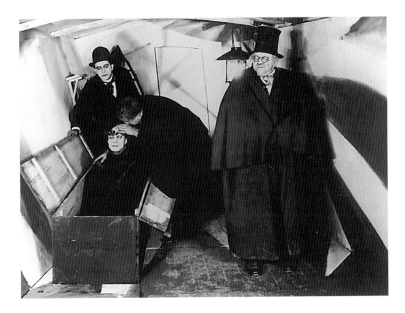

PICTURE: *Black screen*
(from which in the next moments the following light-effects develop:)
(a) a green light-ray (Moon)
(b) a curtain in the transparency of the Moonlight, which becomes brighter
(c) a shadowy hunt behind the curtain:
(d) light and shadow race in confusion. In the whirl, a luridly illuminated arm with a reflecting, flashing dagger plunges down, as a figure raises itself to resist.
Struggle!!!
(e) SLOW FADE TO A BLACK SCREEN AGAIN.

In this act, the finished film follows the script quite faithfully, though with some simplification and a couple of significant additions. The town clerk is no longer identified by name. Franzis and Alan do not walk through the town, or pass the official on his way to the printers, but are found already in the fairground. Both scenes with the rogue (Jakob Straat in the script) have been cut completely: the character will now not make an appearance until Act III. Cesare does not appear outside the booth – only the banner with his Expressionist portrait. Cesare's box is neither 'coffin-like' nor secured by locks: it looks rather like an Italian Futurist construction.

The scene of Cesare's awakening remains one of cinema's most unforgettable sequences. Although the film retains the spirit of the written description, it both simplifies and enriches the effect. When the box is opened, Cesare's eyes are tightly shut. His physical effort is now concentrated not on the fight for breath but on

Franzis and Dr Olfen (Rudolph Lettinger) examine Cesare in Caligari's caravan the struggle to open his eyes, culminating in the ever-haunting moment when the huge, staring, anguished orbs are revealed in their full phenomenal extent. Nor does Cesare now weaken and fall. Gently guided by Caligari's short pointer-stick, he extends his lower arms, and takes a few effortful, robotic steps forward. The scene of Alan's question and Cesare's response follows the script directions, gesture by gesture.

When Franzis and Alan meet Jane on their way from the fairground she is on foot, not in a carriage. They accompany her, walking on either side. There is no 'country house in a park beside a river'. The film cuts instead to a short scene of Caligari's caravan: he emerges from the door, looks around and returns inside. Neither this scene – clearly designed simply to cover the passage of time – nor the next is anticipated in the script. A title 'Heimweg' ('The way home') introduces Franzis and Alan in the night street, having evidently just left Jane, and on the point of parting for the night. Franzis says (title): 'Alan, we both love her.' Alan sighs deeply and looks unhappy. Franzis continues, 'We will leave the choice to her. But we shall stay friends, however her choice may fall.'

In the sequence of the murder of Alan, the preliminary scene of Alan's return to his room and his communion with the night air has been omitted. A title 'Nacht' ('Night') introduces Alan asleep in his bed. On the wall, a man's shadow rises up. Alan wakens, jumps up and extends his arms defensively. As a shadow on the wall, we see the intruder seizing Alan's outstretched hands, then raising a dagger and plunging it into his body. The scene is followed, as directed, by a long blackout. Sadly we never discover what the writers had in mind with their instruction 'a green light-ray (Moon)'. Probably Wiene was as puzzled and defeated by its significance, in the script for a black-and-white film, as we remain today.

ACT III
Scenario
Title: Next morning.[21]
A gaunt old woman – Allan's landlady – runs frantically through the streets, intermittently crossing herself. She arrives at Francis' house, agitatedly knocks and rings the bell, and goes up to Francis' room, to tell him 'Herr Francis–! Herr Francis!! – Young Herr Alland is – dead!'.

Francis accompanies her to her house. In Allan's room he searches for clues.
He goes to the police station to report the affair.
From the police station he goes to the house of Medical Adviser Olfens, Jane's father. Staggering and tearful, he breaks the news to the shocked Jane, then goes to see her father in his surgery.
Calligaris' caravan. Calligaris peers through the window.
Inside, he prepares food on a stove for the somnolent Caesare, whom he feeds with a spoon. Calligaris is startled and annoyed by the arrival of Francis and Olfens, and only reluctantly and angrily lets them enter the caravan. A narrative title informs us assiduously that

Dr Olfens confronted Calligaris and forcefully demanded that he wake the somnambulist. While we battled with Calligaris in this way, a sensational event occurred in another part of Holstenwall which might bring some light into the dark happenings.

In a street on the outskirts of Holstenwall stands a 'curved and twisted house', with an ordinary house in front of it. Suddenly a first-floor window opens and an old woman leans out, shouting 'Murder! Murder!'. Neighbouring windows open and people gaze out. Jakob Straat leaps out of a window, holding a dagger. People give chase. Straat is caught and the dagger taken from him. Some of the crowd want to lynch him, but he is dragged to the police station and brought before the commissioner.

Meanwhile in the caravan, Calligaris looks on angrily as Olfens tries in vain to wake Caesare.

Please wake the somnambule, it is necessary for the investigation.
I regret that Caesare will not wake now.

At this moment, Francis hears, through the window of the caravan, the news of Straat's arrest. Francis and Olfens leave the caravan, hastily read the newspaper, and leave Calligaris, who grins after them, mocking them with deep bows before re-entering the caravan.

The film follows this narrative with only minor changes. The landlady's scenes are curtailed, cutting straight from the street to Franzis' room. The scene scripted for Act II, with Jakob Straat lurking around the night streets, has been inserted before the scene of the woman shouting out of the window (the other window-watchers have been omitted). The script's titles have been drastically cut: the narrative in this act is now practically all visual.

The scenes with the rogue (Jakob Straat) have been separated into two sequences, one of his apprehension, the other of his arrival at the police station. The first now precedes the scene of Caligari feeding Cesare; the second is cut into the caravan scene at the point where Caligari allows Franzis and Olfen to enter the caravan. This rearrangement conveniently covers the time lapses between Franzis and Olfen's decision to go in search of Caligari and their arrival at the caravan; between the rogue's apprehension and the arrival at the police station; and between Franzis and Olfen's entry into the caravan and their attempts to wake the somnambulist.

ACT IV
Scenario
A title explains,

While we now went to the police station for the examination of Jakob Straat, Jane became worried about our long absence and went to look for us at the fairground.

Jane leaves her house and goes to the market place where she sees the newspaper headlines announcing the apprehension of Jakob Straat. A further redundant title tells us

> *Jane wished to bring us the important news quickly and looked for us at Calligaris' Cabinet, while we were involved in the examination of Jakob Straat.*

In the police station, Straat vehemently denies any connection with the two murders. The commissioner does not believe him. Francis however energetically states his belief in Straat's story, and Olfens begins to come round to the same view.

Meanwhile at the fairground, Jane seeks out Calligaris' booth. When she asks Calligaris if her father has been there, the Doctor is very friendly – even fatherly. He shows her the posters of Caesare, and takes her inside the booth. There he unlocks Caesare's box, and wakes the somnambulist. Caesare stares at Jane, betraying 'something like a new emotion'. Jane cannot take her eyes from him, but then 'cringes, takes fright and runs out of the room, to Calligaris' evident amusement.

A title explains that Jane and Francis were reunited at midday, as 'together we were accompanying our poor friend on his last journey.' In the old chapel of a cemetery outside Holstenwall, Allan's funeral is taking place. Afterwards Francis and Jane remain behind, in sad, contemplative silence. From the end of the cemetery avenue, a 'bright, hazy shadow' is seen slowly approaching. It is the ghost of Allan, dressed in the clothes he last wore in his lifetime. The spirit stops beside the couple and gazes affectionately at them. Silently and protectively, Francis leads Jane out into the 'Autumn evening'.

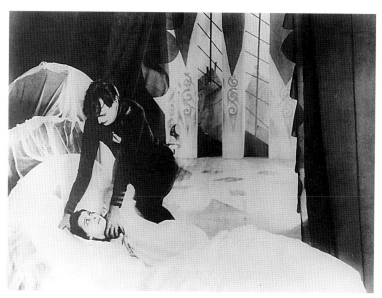

The terrified Jane awakened by Cesare

Calligaris' caravan. The Doctor looks out of the door, then goes back inside, takes Caesare out of his box, and begins to wake him.

Fade.

Francis furtively comes out of the shadows and spies through the window of Calligaris' caravan. Inside he sees Caesare, in his box, amd Calligaris soundly sleeping.

Fade

In the night a shadowy figure makes its way along a garden fence and the wall of Olfens' house.

In her bedroom Jane is sleeping, the moonlight shining through her window.

In Calligaris' caravan the doctor and the somnambulist are still apparently sleeping. Satisfied that all is well, Francis leaves the window and sets off for home.

From this point to the end of the act, it is worth quoting the script verbatim:

20. SCENE: JANE'S BEDROOM.

A shadow appears behind the window (which is draped with a white muslin curtain), and slowly opens the window from outside. The shadow swings over the cill and approaches Jane's bed with mechanical, graceful, rhythmical movements.

21. SCENE: CLOSE-UP

Caesare stands in angular posture by Jane's bed, as she breathes quietly in her sleep. Suddenly as if at a command, Caesare raises his arm, in which a dagger gleams, while his other hand goes to Jane's throat. Jane starts up, giving out wild, terrified shrieks. With arms raised under Caesare's pressure, she manages to fall to her knees and raises her hands in appeal. Caesare stays the hand raised ready to kill, while an agonising struggle plays across his face, on which the merciless stare of bestial stupidity gives way to a lecherous grin. His hand lets go of her throat and seizes Jane's hair, savouring its perfume, then with a greedy hand strokes Jane's body, which quivers profoundly. Caesare's inner struggle lasts for some seconds, then suddenly he is gripped with wild determination, takes her over his arm, throws her over his shoulder, and carries the shrilly shrieking Jane to the window.

FADE

22. SCENE: SERVANTS' ROOM

Two servants are asleep in bed; the older, whitehaired one suddenly starts up, leaps out of bed, wakes the other, they dress and go to the door.

23. SCENE: JANE'S BEDROOM

The window curtain is torn down. The servants rush in together, find Jane's bed empty, her shrieks can be heard from outside. Servants and chambermaid hurl themselves to the window and point with hands upraised in horror into the surrounding grounds, while the doctor, rushing in, collapses for a moment on Jane's bed, and then collects himself with recovered strength and rapidly takes command, as servants with flaming torches leap over the window-cill.

24. SCENE: COURTYARD BEHIND THE HOUSE

The shot shows the [outside of the] window, with the servants standing at the balustrade, and a few metres from them, in the shelter of a right-angled connecting *outbuilding, Caesare, with Jane still over his shoulder. After a brief pause, Caesare lets himself over the rear balustrade, along with his burden. At once the pursuers follow him along the building and over the balustrade. Olfens directs the pursuers from the window.*

25. SCENE: DARK PATH THROUGH FIELDS

Caesare, with Jane still in his arms, rushes along the path, followed by three servants brandishing torches.

26. SCENE: CROOKED PATH IN FIELD

Bushes. Caesare's strength is failing. He drags himself with terrible physical effort, but still laboriously pushes on. The pursuers are closing in; he can no longer carry Jane. She slips from his enfeebled arms and lies helpless, while he hurries onwards.

27. SCENE: FIELD PATH LINED WITH BUSHES

Caesare struggles with his last strength into the bushes, where he collapses.

28: SCENE: AS 26

The pursuers reach Jane, lift her and take her back, while two servants continue after Caesare.

29. SCENE: AS 27

Caesare lies in his last convulsive twitches, breathing with difficulty. Suddenly he stretches one last time, and lies rigid on the ground. The servants rush by, without seeing him in his hiding place, concealed by the darkness.

Jane is taken home, where Francis is waiting. As she recovers consciousness she murmurs, 'It was Caesare!' Francis rushes off with a servant, to warn the police.

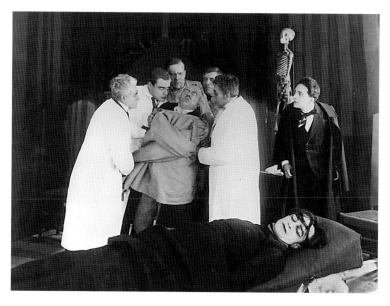

Caligari is put into a strait-jacket ... but only, according to the epilogue, in Franzis' fantasy   6 9

The realised film simplifies the opening of the act. A single, simple title, 'Anxious about her father's long absence …' introduces a shot of Jane reading. Clearly agitated, she puts down her book and stands up decisively. The scene cuts directly to the police station and the examination of the rogue.

The funeral scene is reduced to a single shot of Franzis, Jane and Olfen leaving the cemetery, introduced by a title, 'After the burial'.

The following scene, of Franzis arriving to watch Caligari and Cesare, is more elaborate than in the script. The initial shot of Caligari peering around his caravan is omitted. Now, introduced by the title 'Nacht', Franzis is seen descending the twisted path to the fairground. In the fairground, he peers into Caligari's tent; then arrives at the caravan, to spy through the window.

The scene of Jane's abduction now opens with a shot of Jane asleep in her bed. There are no muslin curtains – possibly since the Expressionist decor offers no convenient fixing!

Generally the action follows the script, though there are significant changes to scene 21. Now Cesare raises his dagger, then freezes. A close-up shows his face serene, perhaps adoring. Very slowly and gently he lowers his hand as if to touch Jane's hair. Only when she wakens, screams and struggles do his expression and action change to brutality and he violently struggles to overpower her and take her up in his arms. Now he seems like some docile animal angered by sudden fear rather than the lecherous rapist suggested by the script.

Cesare's flight with the abducted Jane is extended by two scenes not anticipated in the script. In one of these Cesare carries Jane up a strange angled parapet – quite out of keeping with the topography of the rest of the film and clearly introduced only because it is visually effective (it is remarkably close to a stage setting by Ludwig Sievert for a 1920 production of Kleist's *Penthesilea*, which may itself have been influenced by *Caligari*). The second new scene takes him through an alley in the town. The return to Franzis spying on the apparently sleeping occupants of the caravan is introduced between these two shots, rather than earlier. In Scene 28, instead of two servants, no less than eleven men in dark coats and hats set off in the renewed pursuit of Cesare: the chase seems to have gathered reinforcements like a traditional early film comedy.

The script's scene 29 is wholly omitted; instead the film cuts to a third shot of Franzis watching Caligari's caravan and then making off, to appear immediately afterwards in the subsequent scene of the rescued Jane being revived from her swoon. When Jane announces that her abductor was Cesare, Franzis is insistent that it could not be: '… I watched for hours'. Jane, with an energy that suggests an admirably speedy and complete recovery, insists upon her story. Franzis, persuaded, leaves abruptly.

ACT V
Scenario.
At the police station, Francis is taken to visit a basement cell, to be reassured that Jakob Straat is still held securely. Straat sits disconsolately on his plank bed.

*The commissioner and a number of policemen accompany Francis to Calligaris'
caravan. The lights are out, and Francis and the commissioner knock. When Calligaris
opens the door, he is seized and held by the police. Angry but defiant he points out that
Caesare is secure in his box. Francis has the police carry the box outside and open it up. He
seizes the body in the box: it is only a stuffed dummy.*

*In the confusion that ensues, Calligaris escapes and flees. Francis follows him through
the outskirts of Holstenwall and a landscape with trees. Calligaris leaps into a cab, and
Francis follows him in another. Arriving at a big building, Calligaris gets out of the cab
and disappears inside. The pursuing Francis discovers that the building is a mental hospital.*

*Francis enters the hospital in search of the vanished Calligaris. He tells his story to
some doctors, who take him to see the director of the asylum, who they say has just returned.
He enters the office of the director to find behind the desk - Calligaris himself.*

*Leaving the office, Francis despatches a telegram to Olfens, telling him he is on the
track of Calligaris; and relates the experiences of the past week to the astonished doctors.*

Again the film simplifies the narrative as described by the script. During the
investigation at his caravan, Caligari is never held. Instead he watches apprehensively
as the police carry out Cesare's box. While Franzis and the police open up the box to
reveal the dummy, Caligari easily slips away.

Franzis pursues the doctor on foot up a series of fantastic inclined paths. There
are no cabs: Caligari simply slips into a doorway, followed by Franzis, who pauses only
to read the sign on the door through which Caligari has already disappeared.

The film also gives Franzis more believable reactions than the script indicates.
Suddenly faced in the hospital director's office by Caligari he expresses predictable
horror and panic, and rushes out. Back in the hospital hall, he collapses with shock,
whereupon the doctors rush to help him, giving him the opportunity to tell them his
story. There is no incident of his sending a telegram to summon Jane's father.

The film here adopts a different act division from the script. Act V is extended
from this point, to take in a substantial part of the scriptwriters' Act VI. This achieves
a better balance between the shortened Act V and the (as scripted) over-long Act VI,
and also, as will appear, gives a much stronger climactic end to the act.

ACT VI
Scenario
*Outside the hospital Director's villa, Francis and three doctors wait for a pre-arranged
signal light to tell them when the Director is safely sleeping.*

*In the hospital, they enter the Director's workroom, close the Venetian blinds, and
switch on the electric lights. Francis searches the desk and a young doctor empties a
cupboard, but they find nothing. Then one of the doctors discovers a concealed safe, filled
with books and documents. The script specifies a closeup of the group's heads in a half-circle
– 'Die Köpfe in Halbkreis' – as they study the books. One of these is an eighteenth-century
work on somnambulism, and the doctors confirm that this subject has been a life-long study
for the Director. Reading the book, they find a passage which describes the activities of a*

mystic named Dr. Calligaris, who travelled the fairs of upper Italy in 1723 with a somnambulist called Caesare whom he caused to commit murders under hypnotic influence. He also created a wax figure to serve as an alibi when Caesare was absent on his dreadful business.

Francis and the doctors turn to another document – the Director's own diary. Here they discover an entry saying that while he was still struggling with the study of 'my old problem' he was informed that a somnambulist had been admitted to the hospital.

The manuscript text of the diary fades to a flashback scene set in the Director's workroom. The Director is working behind his desk, when Caesare is brought in in a wheelchair. The Director dismisses the attendants and examines the new patient with growing excitement.

A further diary entry ('4 March … 4 am') exults that he has finally achieved his life's wish of discovering the 'psychiatric secret' of the story of Calligaris, 'how a somnambulist can become simply a mechanical death machine for its client'.

Title: 'Zwangsvorstellungen!!!' ('Hallucination!!!' or 'Obsession!!!'?)

The Director is seen in close-up, poring over his book. His look becomes wilder; and the dark pages of text are overlaid with luminous letters spelling out:

You must become Calligaris and send the somnambulist to kill. Only thus can you serve science.

The Director tries to rid himself of this frightful vision, but in the evening light the message reappears against the dark curtains. He goes out into the park, and sees the message on the trees, 'Du musst Calligaris werden!' ('You must become Calligaris!').

He flees to an outhouse at the edge of the park and leans against the blank wall, his hands raised. Still the message is there.

A transformation comes over the Director. Suddenly he begins to laugh, and to chase the letters of the message like a child playing. He catches the letters one by one, juggles with them and puts them into his pocket, which he pats contentedly.

A title sums up the sequel:

The unhappy scholar was thus possessed by his obsession and now reconstructed with the typical pedantry of scientists, that little Italian story... He prepared a wax figure of the somnambulist, planned a journey and set out on his way.

. . . .

In the Director's work-room, Francis and the doctors are still sitting over the books as the light of dawn enters the window. Francis is called to the telephone: it is Dr Olfens, with news of the fate of Caesare.

In the field where he died, Caesare's corpse is discovered by Dr Olfens and police officials.

In the park of the asylum, Francis greets Olfens and the police commissioner, who arrive with a covered stretcher.

In the corridor outside the Director's room, Francis, Olfens, the commissioner and the doctors, accompanied by the stretcher, arrive at the door of the Director's work room. They knock.

TITLE: *'Good morning, Herr Dr. Calligaris ... Caesare died by his last murder attempt.'*

The Director – now definitively identified as Calligaris – gets up from his desk. Francis snatches the cover from the stretcher to reveal the corpse of Caesare. Calligaris is suddenly broken by shock and grief.

The once passionate expression is gone; the men lead out of the room a childish, feeble-minded idiot, a giggling dotard.
FADE
In a hospital cell the now feeble-minded Calligaris is placed in a barred cot.
SLOW FADE OUT AND IN.
On the place where Calligaris' booth stood, a plaque has been placed on a wooden post. The inscription reads:
    Here stood the cabinet of Dr Calligaris.
    Peace to his victims. Peace to him!
    The Town of Holstenwall.
Francis and Jane stand before the plaque, deep in thought.

The scenes as scripted, up to the Director/Caligari's vision of the luminous message, now form the concluding part of the film's Act V. The discovery of the documents and the flashback to the arrival of Cesare as a patient in the hospital follow the script directions closely, apart from two brief cut-in shots of the Director sleeping in his bed. The flashback action is elaborated after the Director has dismissed the attendants: he eagerly studies his book, then throws it away and joyously embraces the sleeping Cesare.

The message 'Du musst Caligari werden' is now introduced in a title attributed to the Director's own thoughts. The device of the luminous letters is reduced to a single appearance, superimposed on the wall of the outside storehouse. Sadly, no doubt for reasons of technical difficulty, the inspired notion of having the Director/Caligari catch and pocket the individual letters of the message has been dropped completely.

Act VI of the finished film opens with the return to Franzis and the doctors, still poring over the Director's diary. From this point the narrative is simplified. There is no telephone call to Dr Olfen, who makes no further appearance in the film. A messenger comes in to Franzis and the doctors to inform them that 'the sleeper' has been found. In the next shot Franzis joins the men who were seen in pursuit of Cesare in Act IV, as they stand over the somnambulist's corpse in the field where he collapsed.

Franzis and the doctors arrive in the corridor outside the Director's room with a covered stretcher. Franzis bursts into the Director's office. 'Take off the mask. You are Caligari.' Caligari is startled but still truculent. The stretcher is brought in. Franzis snatches off the cover. Caligari, suddenly shocked and broken, falls upon the body of Cesare, then straightens up, raving. He is put into a strait-jacket and taken to another room, where, seen in medium close shot, he appears to succumb to exhaustion. Franzis watches as the door is closed on Caligari.

The epilogue is entirely different from the script. An iris-in on Franzis's face is followed immediately by an iris out into the same set-up as the opening scene of the film: Franzis on a bench with the wild-eyed listener. Franzis concludes his story: 'And since that day the madman has never left his cell.'

The two men go into the courtyard of what we now see is the asylum, where a dozen people are behaving in clearly disturbed fashion. Franzis points out Cesare, caressing a bunch of flowers, and goes over to Jane, who gazes vacantly into the distance. He asks her to marry him. She replies, 'We Queens are not free to follow our hearts.'

The Director enters the courtyard. He has now the appearance of a respectable, kindly bourgeois, without the wild hair, the spectacles and the fiendish grin of Caligari. Franzis attacks him, screaming 'You all believe that I am mad! It is not true – the Director is mad!!' 'He is Caligari, Caligari, Caligari!'. Attendants seize Franzis and secure him in a strait-jacket. The director examines him closely, then puts on his spectacles and declares encouragingly,

At last I understand his delusion. He takes me for that mystic Caligari. And now I also know the way to his cure.

END

NOTES

· ·

1 Siegfried Kracauer, *From Caligari to Hitler: A Psychological History of the German Film* (Princeton, N.J.: Princeton University Press, 1947).

2 Written about 1941, the typescript is now in the Billy Rose Theatre Collection, at New York Public Library. Parts of it are published as an appendix to Mike Budd (ed.), *The Cabinet of Dr Caligari: Texts, Contexts, Histories* (New Brunswick and London: Rutgers University Press, 1990).

3 Franz Janowitz left a posthumous volume of poems, *On the Earth*. Hans Janowitz wrote that his brother had 'uselessly bled to death for the benefit of a shameful government for which he felt nothing but contempt ... I have never been able since to trust the authoritative power of an inhuman state gone mad'. In Hans Janowitz, 'Caligari: The Story of a Famous Story'.

4 Rolf Hempel, *Carl Mayer. Ein Autor schreibt mit der Kamera* (Berlin: Henschelverlag Kunst und Gesellschaft, 1968).

5 Siegbert S. Prawer has sought a work of this title without success. He reports a reference elsewhere in Stendhal's correspondence, however, to a son and pupil of Veronese known as Carlo Caliari; and also points out the Italian place-name Cagliari. Prawer, 'Von "Filmroman" zum Kinofilm' in *Das Cabinet des Dr. Caligari. Drehbuch von Carl Mayer und Hans Janowitz* (Berlin: Stiftung Deutsche Kinemathek, 1995).

6 Janowitz ('Caligari: The Story of a Famous Story') says that they had previously telephoned Pommer and made an appointment for four o'clock the same day. This is the more likely version, given the unreliability of most of Pommer's stories.

7 In 'Caligari: The Story of a Famous Story' Janowitz boasts, apparently without justification, that the sum was 6,500 marks, with the promise of a further 2,000 when (or rather if) the film went into production, and 1,000 more in the (at that point) improbable circumstance of the film being sold for foreign release.

8 'Ein Brief von Fritz Lang', in Walter Kaul (ed.), *Caligari und Caligarismus* (Berlin: Deutsche Kinemathek Berlin, 1970), p. 23.

9 Janowitz ('Caligari: The Story of a Famous Story') regarded it as a further asset that Wiene's father, the actor Carl Wiene, had 'gone slightly mad when he could no longer appear on the stage'.

10 Hermann Warm, 'Gegen die Caligari-Legenden' in Kaul (ed.), *Caligari und Caligarismus*, pp. 11-16.

11 Budd (ed.), *The Cabinet of Dr Caligari*.

12 Could the writers' insistence on Mayer's reading the script to Pommer have been because they were initially reluctant to let him see such an untidy document?

13 Lotte Eisner wrote that Kubin's 'obsessed works seem to arise from a chaos of light and shadow. Kubin's *Caligari* would certainly have been full of Goyaesque visions ... In a half-autobiographical, half-fantastic tale, *Die Andere Seite*, published in 1922, he describes his wanderings through the dark streets, possessed by an obscure force which led him to imagine weird houses and landscapes, terrifying or grotesque situations ... It is a pity that so vivid a painter of nightmares was never commissioned for *Caligari*'. In Lotte Eisner, *The Haunted Screen* (London: Thames and Hudson, 1967).

14 Paul Rotha, *The Film Till Now* (London: Jonathan Cape, 1930; London: Vision – Mayflower, 1949, 1951, 1960, 1963).

15 Erich Pommer, 'Carl Mayer's Debut', in *A Tribute to Carl Mayer 1894-1944* (London: programme for a memorial show to Carl Mayer held at the Scala Theatre, 13 April 1947).

16 Hermann Warm, 'Gegen die Caligari-Legenden', in Kaul (ed.), *Caligari und Caligarismus*, pp. 11-16.

17 Warm, 'Gegen die Caligari-Legenden'. Teasingly Warm gives us no indication of the source of this opposition.

18 'Against Lang's protests, shooting [of Part II of *Die Spinnen*] was not begun until the autumn .... and because of bad weather

conditions filming had to be transferred
from the Hagenbeck grounds to the studio.'
Eisner, *The Haunted Screen*.

19 Warm, 'Gegen die Caligari-Legenden',
pp. 11-16.

20 Walter Kaul, 'Bestandsaufnahme 70:
Nicht nur Expressionistisch und caligaresk',
in Kaul (ed.), *Caligari und Caligarismus*, p. 6.

21 Added in manuscript.

22 Significantly, these were the dimensions
of Georges Méliès' studio stage at
Montreuil, Paris. Deutsches Bioscop
GmbH's Berlin studio, built a year before
Weissensee, was 9 x 6 metres.

23 Letter dated 17 January 1970, published
as 'Ein Brief von Fritz Lang' in Kaul (ed.),
Caligari und Caligarismus, p. 23

24 Ibid.

25 Janowitz, 'Caligari: The Story of a
Famous Story'.

26 Kracauer, *From Caligari to Hitler*.

27 Ibid.

28 Eisner, *The Haunted Screen*.

29 In *Berlin Börsen-Kurier*, 29 February 1920;
cited in Kaul (ed.), *Caligari und Caligarismus*.

30 Eisner, *The Haunted Screen*.

31 Edouard Beaucamp, 'Art et vie.
Métamorphose de l'Expressionisme', in
Paris Berlin 1900-1933 (Paris: Centre
national d'art et de culture Georges
Pompidou, 1978).

32 Stephanie Barron, *German Expressionism
1915-1925. The Second Generation* (Los
Angeles: Los Angeles County Museum of
Art, 1988).

33 John Willett, *Expressionism* (London:
Weidenfeld and Nicholson – World
University Library, 1970).

34 *Der Sohn*, at that time prohibited by the
official censorship, was first produced in a
private performance in Dresden by Ernst
Deutsch, the actor friend of Janowitz.

35 Introduction to catalogue of the
exhibition 'Deutscher Expressionismus
Darmstadt' cited in Barron (ed.), *German
Expressionism*.

36 Cf. Prawer's essay, 'Von "Filmroman"
zum Kinofilm', in *Das Cabinet des Dr.

*Caligari. Drehbuch von Carl Mayer und Hans
Janowitz zu Robert Wienes Film von 1919/20*.

37 Reproduced in Budd (ed.), *The Cabinet
of Dr Caligari*.

38 Werner Krauss, *Das Schauspiel meines
Lebens* (Stuttgart: Goverts, 1952), pp. 78-9.

39 'Der beseelte und der psychologische
Mensch', in *Das Junge Deutschland*, 1918;
cited and translated in Richard Samuel and
R. Hinton Thomas, *Expressionism in
German Life, Literature and the Theatre*
(Cambridge: Cambridge University Press,
1939).

40 By the end of the First World War
German production was second only to
Hollywood; in 1921 Germany made 246
features while France produced 74 and
Britain 44.

41 Thomas Elsaesser, 'Social Mobility and
the Fantastic: German Silent Cinema', in
James Donald (ed.), *Fantasy and the Cinema*
(London: BFI, 1989); reprinted in Budd
(ed.), *The Cabinet of Dr Caligari*.

42 Quoted in George Huaco, *The Sociology
of Film Art* (New York: Basic Books, 1965),
p. 34.

43 *The German Cinema* (London: J. M.
Dent and Sons, 1971).

44 Budd (ed.), *The Cabinet of Dr Caligari*.

45 'The Screen', *New York Times*, 4 April
1921, p. 5.

46 Budd (ed.), *The Cabinet of Dr Caligari*.

47 Even in the larger theatres of that time,
the pressures on cinema orchestras rarely
permitted even one complete rehearsal
before the first performance of a film.

48 *Musical America*, vol. 33, no. 25, 16
April 1921, p. 5, quoted in George C. Pratt,
*Spellbound in Darkness. A History of the
Silent Film* (Rochester, New York:
University of Rochester, 1966).

49 'The Screen', *New York Times*, 4 April
1921, p. 5.

50 Kristin Thompson, 'Dr Caligari at the
Folies-Bergère, or, The Successes of an
Early Avant-Garde Film', in Budd (ed.),
The Cabinet of Dr Caligari; David B. Pratt,
'"Fit Food for Madhouse Inmates" The Box

Office Reception of the German Invasion of 1921', in *Griffithiana* 48/49 (Gemona: Cineteca di Friuli), October 1993, pp. 97-157.
51 Ibid.
52 This translation was originally published in the English-language periodical *Broom* (Rome), 4 July 1922.
53 Jean Epstein, quoted in René Jeanne and Charles Ford, *Histoire Encyclopaedique du Cinéma, II. Le Cinéma muet (suite)* (Paris: S.E.D.E., 1953), p. 152.
54 Written in 1923 and quoted in René Clair, *Réflexion faite: notes pour servir à l'histoire de l'art cinématographique de 1920 à 1950* (Paris: Gallimard, 1951).

55 Rotha, *The Film Till Now.*
56 Lewis Jacobs, *The Rise of the American Film. A Critical History* (New York: Harcourt, Brace and Company, 1939), pp. 303-5
57 Richard J. Murphy, 'Carnival Desire and the Sideshow of Fantasy: Dream, Duplicity and Representational Instability' in *The Cabinet of Dr. Caligari*, in *The Germanic Review*, Winter 1991, pp. 45–56. Despite his confusion over the narrative content of the film, Murphy offers some interesting reflections on the persistent theme of sleep in *Caligari*.

CREDITS

....

Das Cabinet des Dr. Caligari. Filmschauspiel in 6 Akten

Germany
1920
Production company
Decla-Film Gesellschaft.
Holz & Co.
German première
26 February 1920,
Marmorhaus, Berlin
US première
3 April 1921, Capitol
Theatre, 51st and
Broadway, New York
French première
3 March 1922, Ciné-Opera,
Paris
British première
17 March 1924
Production
Erich Pommer
Rudolph Meinert
Director
Robert Wiene
Scenario
Carl Mayer, Hans Janowitz
Photography
Willy Hameister
Editor
not credited
Designers
Hermann Warm
Walter Reimann
Walter Röhrig
**Musical score
for original Berlin
presentation**
Giuseppe Becce
**Musical director
at original Berlin
presentation**
Leo Zelinsky
Length of film
1703 metres

Werner Krauss
*Dr. Caligari/Director of
asylum*
Conrad Veidt
Cesare
Lil Dagover
Jane
Friedrich Feher
Franzis
**Hans-Heinz von
Twardowski**
Alan
Rudolph Lettinger
Dr Olfen
Ludwig Rex
a rogue
Elsa Wagner
landlady
Henri Peters-Arnolds
Hans Lanser-Ludolff

Credits checked by Markku
Salmi

The newly restored and
colour tinted print of *Das
Cabinet des Dr. Caligari* in
the National Film and
Television Archive was
acquired for the 360 Classic
Feature Films project from
the BundesArchiv –
FilmArchiv, Koblenz.

NOTE: The title of the film
still frequently occurs in
print (even in Lotte Eisner's
The Haunted Screen) as *Das
Kabinett des Dr Caligari*.
The earliest appearance of
the title, on the script by
Mayer and Janowitz, is as
*Das Cabinet des Dr.
Calligaris*, but with the
name amended in ink to
Calligari on the title page
and throughout much (but
not all) of the script. On the
contract of 19 April 1920,
the title appears as *Das
Kabinett des Dr. Calligari*.
Preliminary newspaper
advertisements, in January
1920, use the form *Das
Kabinett des Dr. Kaligari*.
On the film itself, and in all
publicity at the time of
actual release, the title
appears as *Das Cabinet des
Dr. Caligari*, with a 'C' for
Cabinet, a single 'T' at the
end of the word, and a full
stop after 'Dr.' This was
apparently the final decision
of the writers: in his 1941
typescript, Janowitz recalls
the anxious debates that led
to it, 'We discussed the
Caligari orthography and
decided to write his name
with a "C", for any other
way would have been
completely wrong. But
"Kabinett" with a "K"?
Whether "Caligari" were to
be spelled with one or two
"l's" called for an extended
debate, over which we fell
asleep.' Several
contemporary reviewers
however used the spelling
'Kabinett', as did Hermann
Warm in his recollections
of the film half a century
later.